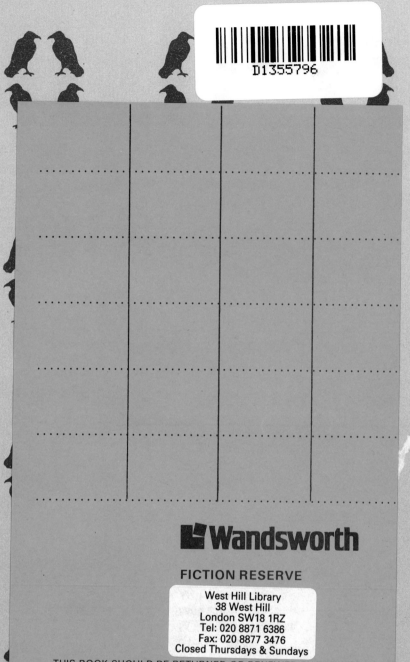

THE ARMED HANDS

FR ROLFE
BARON CORVO

The Armed Hands
and other stories and pieces

EDITED AND
WITH AN INTRODUCTION BY
CECIL WOOLF

1974
CECIL & AMELIA WOOLF
LONDON

ROLF

100525780

Copyright © 1974 by Cecil Woolf
Published by Cecil & Amelia Woolf
Kingly Court, 10 Kingly Street, London WIA 4ES
Printed in Great Britain by The Anchor Press Ltd
Tiptree, Essex
Endpapers by Neil J. Crawford
after an original design by the author

ISBN 0 900821 13 2

Contents

* Previously unpublished pieces are marked with an asterisk.

7

Introduction

This volume contains a selection from Rolfe's uncollected stories, sketches, essays, books reviews and miscellaneous writings over a period of twenty-three years. Although the sixteen pieces are of a highly diverse character, they seem to me worth gathering together, since only two have appeared in covers and seven have never yet been printed. A further reason for publication, despite their somewhat fragmentary and miscellaneous character, is that they indicate a wider range of interest, theme and style than is generally attributed to Rolfe.

The thread connecting most of the pieces is an element of autobiography, which is present in nearly all Rolfe's work. A distinction must be made, however, between the various forms this autobiography takes. In his introduction to Rolfe's *Hubert's Arthur* A.J.A.Symons wrote of its author: 'Two main tendencies are exhibited in his work: a subjective capacity to project himself into fictional autobiography as a form of dream compensation for his unhappy life, and an objective dramatization of past history.' Such a distinction is pertinent, but oversimplified. It is debatable whether Rolfe's treatment of history was 'objective', and Symons's formulation takes no account of a more important distinction – between the various forms which the 'subjective capacity to project himself into fictional autobiography' take. Essentially there are three forms – straight autobiography, wish fulfilment or fantasy, and the actual creation of events as material for his work.

Ostensibly fiction, *Arrested as a Spy* is in fact pure autobiography. Judging from two postcards to his friend Harry Pirie-Gordon, it is an unvarnished account of an incident which occurred during Rolfe's first year in Venice. The untitled sketch printed here as *The Venetians* dates from his last year there, and it is interesting to note that after the trials of five years' residence several of the author's illusions about the Venetians had come to grief. Another story, *Temptation*, which was almost certainly based on direct personal

8

experience, brings out a different aspect of Rolfe's character – his compassionate concern for others. The piece from which the title of this volume is drawn and the Rolfean *jeu d'esprit* entitled *The Bull Against the Enemy of the Anglican Race* both belong to the category of wish fulfilment or fantasy. Lord Northcliffe's unforgivable sin, against which Rolfe in his role of Hadrian VII thunders his bull of excommunication, is that he symbolizes the cheap Press and all the developments in Fleet Street during the nineties. As Shane Leslie has written, 'it is doubtful if the Latinists of the Roman Bullarium could have composed anything so sustained, furious, and magnificently medieval'. In *The Armed Hands* Rolfe is again indulging in wish fulfilment and fantasy. The extraordinary 'slight Grey Man', who wreaks such havoc in Edwardian Oxford, is obviously himself as he would wish to be. Symons recalled that Rolfe wore a strange ring on his hand, 'in which a small spur was mounted on a bezel. This, he explained, was for the purpose of protecting himself from kidnapping attempts, and he wore it in consequence of an assault on his person made years before by the Jesuits. When they essayed, as he fully expected, a further abduction, he would sweep with his armed hand at the brow of his assailant. A line would thus be scored in the flesh which would draw blood; and his blinded enemy (blinded by the dripping blood) would be at the mercy of the intended victim.' When he chose, Rolfe could write a good short story. *The Armed Hands* shows his love of form, his instinct for clarity and conciseness, and his flair for the dramatic situation. Another story set in Oxford is *In Praise of Billy B.*, which Rolfe published in *The Holywell Record*. Although he does not himself appear to figure in this piece there can be little doubt that the plot and the characters are based on an incident and people well known to Rolfe during his time there as an unattached student.

A very different story, belonging to the Venetian phase of Rolfe's life and closely related in its conception to the early part of his novel *The Desire and Pursuit of the Whole*, is *Daughter of a Doge*. Figuring as Nicholas Crabbe, Rolfe is once again able to blend truth and fantasy. Here, as in the novel, his imagination conceived the boy-girl as a means of legitimizing his sexual inversion, and her descent from a Doge is a naive expression of Rolfe's respect for blood. But the writer transmutes his real-life friendship with the

young Ermenegildo into a strangely convincing character, Zilda.
In another Italian story, set in the countryside near Rome, Rolfe
recalls an incident he learned of during his stay with the elderly
English Duchess Sforza-Cesarini, following his expulsion from the
Scots College. Written in 1891 but not so far published, *Toto* was the
forerunner of a series which attracted wide attention as *Stories Toto
Told Me*.

Another form of autobiographical fiction, and the most interesting of all, is represented here by the remarkable piece called
Excommunicated, where the situation which Rolfe describes is actually
created by himself. The story shows clearly that though his public
writings, as distinct from his correspondence, are often a valuable
source for the events of his life, they need to be consulted with
caution and controlled in the light of other information: for reality
is often subtly coloured and distorted by self-justification. *Excommunicated* is one of several autobiographical stories in which Rolfe
writes of his life in Holywell. Wherever he found himself, he eventually entered into combat and in that obscure Welsh town he found
a new battleground. It is hard to uncover the real source of his rage
against the parish priest, Fr Beauclerk. Ostensibly the quarrel
began as a small matter, a personal disagreement over payment
for work, but for Rolfe it raised important questions and gradually
developed into the most violent of his quarrels. In *Excommunicated*
he tells the story, as he sees it, of his last year in the town.* The
claim he made and genuinely believed – that he had been excommunicated – was without foundation; what in fact he did was
to create such a scene that he found himself deprived of the sacraments. It is unlikely that anyone whose relations were as bad as
Rolfe's with Fr Beauclerk would feel able to present himself either
for confession or communion. So that as long as he remained in the
parish the sacraments were available to him only in theory.
Eventually the matter came to the notice of the bishop, who saw
Rolfe personally and signified his displeasure. He left without
giving Rolfe his blessing and this probably explains why Rolfe
believed he was excommunicate. There is a curious sequel to this
episode in a letter in which Rolfe relates how two years later a friend

* For a less partisan account of what has aptly been called the Battle of Holywell,
the reader may turn to A.J.A. Symons's *The Quest for Corvo*, or his brother Julian
Symons's article in *The Saturday Book: fifth year*, 1945.

arranged for the bishop to visit him in his Hampstead lodging to straighten things out. The incident was subsequently transmuted into the dramatic scene in *Hadrian the Seventh*, where the cardinal and bishop call at Rose's to ask his forgiveness.

The dividing line between these various forms of autobiographical writing – the straight reportage, the wish fulfilment or fantasy, and the situations he actually creates, as well as the line between fact and fiction – is often ill-defined.

The motives that impelled Rolfe to devote so much ink to writing of himself are clearer: 'I write slowly and with great difficulty', he tells us in his entry for *Who's Who*, and a passage from a letter to him from the popular Catholic novelist and preacher R.H. Benson shows that Rolfe had less than complete confidence in himself as a creative writer: 'You once said to me that plot was your weak point. I think there is a truth in that. What you can do (Good Lord how you can!) is to build up a situation when you have got it. You are a vignette – a portrait – not a landscape painter, a maker of chords not of progressions.' Rolfe's life provides him with a ready situation on which to build. Another motive for projecting himself into his work is to furnish his contemporaries and posterity with the true saga of his life which, as I have shown, he often appears to shape as a basis for his literary work.

Another reason why much of Rolfe's creative output is so intimately concerned with himself is to fulfil a deep psychological need. Throughout his writings Rolfe presents his personality under the guise of various masks, some in the present, some in the past. The historical masks, de Burgh in *Hubert's Arthur* and Dom Gheraldo in *Don Renato*, are narrators or observers, whereas under the masks of George Arthur Rose and Nicholas Crabbe Rolfe not merely dominates the actions in which he appears, but he is the action.

The element of autobiography is never wholly absent from Rolfe's work – prose, poetry and painting. Everything he touches is impregnated with his personality. We have glanced at those writings which are essentially autobiographical. The remaining pieces reflect various aspects of his character. Readers of the novel *Don Renato* will not be surprised to learn that Rolfe showed remarkable interest in a wide variety of matters, great and small. He had an almost schoolboy delight in searching out strange and recondite pieces of information with which to confound readers, friends and correspondents. He revelled in everything to do with the Catholic Church. In 1899 he had written an article for a popular American Sunday newspaper describing the procedure following the death of a pope, with an account of the conclave. *Notes on the Conclave* was written four years later, when Leo XIII was lying on his death bed. Another ecclesiastical piece, written during the short period Rolfe spent at a Roman seminary in 1890, is the remains of a discourse on Daniel's Messianic prophecy. The short article entitled *Concerning England and Germany* reflects the author's intense affection for England which also manifests itself in *Hadrian the Seventh* and elsewhere. His love of Renaissance Italy is represented here by the essay *Suggestion for a Criterion of the Credibility of Certain Historians*. This is a revised version of a lengthy piece intended as an appendix to Rolfe's *Chronicles of the House of Borgia*. 'He defended his own character in whitewashing the Borgias', suggested Symons. Both in the appendix, which was set up in type but omitted from the published work, and in the subsequent version, Rolfe deals with charges of homosexuality made against the Borgia. The three book reviews are perhaps the weakest pieces in this selection – weakest in the sense of being the least special; but nothing of Rolfe's is without interest.

To mark the centenary of his birth I published a volume of essays on various aspects of Rolfe's life and work. In one of these essays Dom Sylvester Houédard asked: '. . . how much longer will it be before . . . we see all extant' material by Rolfe 'published, ephemeral as well as the rest?' This book is an attempt to meet that need.

C.W.

The author's use of square brackets, as distinct from the curved form, has made it necessary to use two styles of square bracket: Rolfe's are printed thus [ ] and the editor's bold brackets thus **[ ]**. All the footnotes are Rolfe's, except those signed 'Ed.'.

The Armed Hands

Life is a grotesque series of magic-lantern pictures: at least, mine is.
I am among a heavily-breathing intense mob, in the dark. Suddenly, the Showman flashes before me a brilliant disc of a picture
quite unrelated to its surroundings. It stays, during a moment – I
don't know how. It means – I can't think what. It vanishes – I
don't know where. And life is as obscurely uninteresting as before –
I haven't a notion why.

For example: I saw three blazingly clear pictures at Oxford in
Eights Week. I make a point of being up during Eights Week,
because (as a physical epicure) I like to see how England's most
recent flesh is coming on. It (as you know) is on view daily, at
16.30 and 18 p.m., on the towing-path between the Osteria Iside
and the barges.

On the first morning, Thursday, I went out for a dawdle before
my coffee. I prowled, for no earthly reason, a little way up the
Via Woodstochiana. Few people are abroad in Oxford at 7 o'clock
of the morn, excepting on the paths which lead to Il Piacere de'
Parocchi. Anyhow, Campo Sant' Egidio and that little bit of Via
Woodstochiana were deserted at that particular moment. As the
first of my three pictures was exhibited in this neighbourhood, it will
be well to precise the spot.

On the left of Via Woodstochiana, the shops ended with a sort of
emporium. Then, there was an alley; and, on the other side of the
alley, a fairly-sizeable plain house. The alley seemed quite an
ordinary stone-paved little slipe. On its south side, was the side-
wall of the dwelling pertaining to the emporium. On its north side,
was the side-wall of the plain house. The front-doors of these two
buildings were not in Via Woodstochiana but in the alley, one
facing the other. In squinting up the alley, I fancied that it led to a
third (but rather more embellished) building. I hope that this is all
clear.

As I turned into the alley from motives of inquisitiveness, I saw a

13

man approaching me. I did not particularly note him at the time, beyond the fact that his face wore the positively indescribable (but saliently recognizable) expression of one who has just prayed well. But he certainly did strike me as being as grey a man as I could wish to see. I don't mean his hair: he was bare-headed, closely-clipped, and slightly bald on the tonsure. And I don't mean his face: that was tanned and healthy enough, and quite in keeping with his slight (but rather broadbreasted) figure and his quietly agile gait. But I mean his perfect poise, and his sedate gravity, which were simply as grey as grey can be. And I mean his clothes. They seemed a symphony of dark-grey tones. Even his watch-chain and key-chain and scarf-pin and sleeve-links had the dark-grey gleam of platinum; and his neat slippers were of dark-grey suede. The white of his collar, the white of the silk-handkerchief in his sleeve and the black of his neck-tie, were just what was wanted to bind his colour-scheme beautifully together. I never in my life have seen a man looking so simply and calmly staid. Indeed, after passing him, – we met midway between the embellished edifice and the two side front-doors which I have mentioned, – I could not help looking back at him. And then, without the very slightest warning, the picture was flashed upon my brain.

This was it. I was well up the alley and looking down it toward Via Woodstochiana. The Grey Man was in the alley between the door of the plain house and the door of the emporium. All of a sudden, both doors slid open inwardly and silently. A thick-set gentleman in glossy black oozed out of the plain house-door; and said something affably to the Grey Man. It seemed also to be civil: but the distance, of course, rendered it inaudible by me. It could not have been more than six words. The Grey Man, without halting, gave a courteously-negative gesture with his head. A burly red-bearded fellow slipped out of the open emporium-door; and began (with the glossy black gentleman) to butt and hustle the Grey Man toward the open door of the plain house. The Grey Man sprang, like a kitten, one pace backward; and instantly rebounded forward, launching a lightning-like right-and-left double-knock – ping-pang, pong-pung – across the two foreheads. Blood splashed out in the most extraordinary manner. I never before saw such gushings. I heard two swiftly-sucked-in breaths and a couple of stifled gasping groans. The assailants, carrying their heads, staggered into their respective houses. The doors shut as noiselessly as they had opened. The Grey Man quite quietly went on his unruffled way.

All this happened while one could count nine. It blazed into vision for nine seconds; and, then, was not. It, indeed, was so amazing, that (for an instant) I believed myself to be the subject of an hallucination. So I stepped back to the mouth of the alley. There were puddles of fresh gore, on the pavement between the doorways. I looked out into Via Woodstochiana. There, was the Grey Man demurely crossing Campo Sant' Egidio by the cabmen's shelter, and going in the direction of the Collegio di San Zanbatista. He went with easy swiftness, his hands in his trousers' pockets. If I had not already noticed him, I certainly should have failed to do so, so accurately did he come with the landscape.

It was excessively queer. I won't deny that I stood and pondered the event, perhaps for a couple of minutes. For the life of me I couldn't understand what I had seen. Still, it obviously was no affair of mine. I thought, however, that I might well postpone exploration of that alley and go home and have my coffee. So I did.

The fourth day after that was Sunday. In the evening I dined with old Sniffles at his house on Muro Lungo. That man's collection of intagliate alexandroliths ought to fetch quite a quarter of a million when he turns up his toes. We spent the whole evening in pawing the gems.

As I mounted my bicycle at his door, at last, a clock announced the half past 23; and all the other timepieces in the city corroborated the statement. Several spoke together, very discordantly: of course there were the usual laggards: but the gist of the testimony was fairly unanimous. As it was a fine night, I resolved to ride a little way before tucking up. The dark darkness of night suits my thinking apparatus better than the light darkness of day – the fat dismal unwieldly ordinary uneventful day. So I went up Via del Santo Pozzo into Via Larga; and turned the corner, intending to ride up Via Banburiana as far as Città Destate and back. Be it always and everywhere and by everyone remembered that I had no reason whatever for this choice of route. It just occurred to me to go that way; and I as simply went.

I suppose that, if the Oxford policemen read this, they will feel bound to lay a trap and run me in. The fact is that, instead of going by road round the fore-court of Collegio di San Zanbatista, I pedalled lazily through the posts and all along the pavement in front of the old college-buildings, just like an ordinary under-graduate at 10 a.m. Not a soul breathed near. Even after I had got through the second set of posts, I did not trouble to leave the pave-ment immediately, but rode along the façade of the new college-buildings, passing the first lamp-post, and only gliding into the road on reaching the second before the administrator's office. And it was here that the second picture unexpectedly glared me in the face.

You understand that I had the Uffizio Amministrativo del Collegio di San Zanbatista on my right hand, and was about to pass the adjoining entry which leads to the college. Beyond this entry was a new-faced Casa Iacopesca joined to a pub which (in turn) attached itself to the row of houses before you come to the Allogio dei Giudici. On my left, stretched the great dim open width and length of Campo Sant' Egidio with its leafy avenues. Before me, the pavement lay like a grey ribbon. There was a fair light on the foreground of it, a light shed by a third lamp-post which stood at the juncture of the Casa Iacopesca and the pub: but, beyond that, the middle distance faded gradually into the night.

Just when I was crawling by the Uffizio Amministrativo of the college, I recognized the Grey Man. He came toward me from the direction of Via Banburiana; and I spotted him as he came into the light of the third lamp-post. Quite instantaneously the double door of the Casa Iacopesca opened like a dumb mouth. Two small ghostly gentlemen pranced out. They both sported black trousers and peculiarly long black jackets agreeably slit up the rear. One was long-bodied and stumpy-legged: the other was grotesquely verdant-greeny: both wore snubbed noses and spectacles. And they, also, set themselves silently to butt and hustle the Grey Man into the blackness of their open door. Then followed the same two hideous crashes of fists upon foreheads, the same two spouting sheets of blood, the same suppressed squeals and unhesitating evanishments, the same slammed speechless door, and the same impassive invulnerable solitary figure pursuing its mysterious way.

Mind you – this time, I was not a couple of yards distant from

16

the collision. The whole thing was begun and finished by the time I had pedalled four times. Nothing could have been smarter. I had not even time to dismount – much less to say something equivalent to 'Ciò!'

I gazed at the Casa Iacopesca. All the windows were blind. There was a glimmer in the bar of the pub beyond: but not a movement anywhere. I looked all round. No one was in sight, excepting the moth-grey figure passing through the posts of San Zanbatista. I very much wanted to run after him. But of course that was out of the question.

And, then, you must know something else. I really was seized (at the moment) with grave doubt concerning my quality of visibility. None of these gladiators seemed to have noticed me at all. They popped out, and did their trick, and scuttled back into their burrow (so to speak), just as though they were quite alone. It was most puzzling, not to say annoying.

The only things which I could think of, to say, in this emergency were 'Mariavergine!' and 'Ostreghette!' I said them alternately to myself half-a-dozen times, observing uncanonical intervals, as I rode up Via Banburiana toward Città Destate; and derived immense relief. Furthermore, just by the Giardini di Norham, a motor-car blasphemed me for riding on the wrong side of the road. This was a vast consolation: for it certified me that I could still be seen.

Some people cannot look at pictures without worrying themselves about the artist's meaning, and rot of that sort. (They are the kind of people who begin their criticisms with the formula 'Ow! I down't lyke the fyce.') Now I always try to look at pictures with a sole purpose of taking my pleasure. But, I admit that the two last exhibitions tried me severely. It was irritating to feel, on the inaccessible back of one's mind, the nipping flea of curiosity. However, I just blundered on toward my grave, through my normal state of mist, till the following Wednesday.

It was the last day of the Eights. The afternoon had been muggy, dully threatening rain. At 17.30 p.m. I took advantage of the interval between the two races to stroll down the towing-path. My idea was to find a place where I might observe the men – not the crews, but the men who run along the bank. I am not aware of any spot on this planet, excepting Venice, which offers a more exhaustive and instructive exhibition of vigorous physique, than this particular bit of Oxford at this particular moment. The show comprises several hundred specimens; and I solemnly aver that one in twenty is quite worth looking at twice. Why not? *Athletam in ingenuum nasci tam facile est quam accedere huc.*

The point, of getting below Ponti Lunghi for the purpose, is this. Shortly before 18 o'clock, the men come down, from the barges and elsewhere, to (say) the Osteria Iside whereby the boats are moored. When the starting-gun fires, they run back (along the towing-path) by the sides of their respective boats. To stand on the towing-path during this process, amounts to competing for being bunted (by roaring gladiators) into a fussy river. But, just below the Ponti Lunghi, the towing-path winds round the Budello; and there is a short cut across the grass from Ponti Lunghi to the point where the path follows the straightened course of the river. And it is possible to preserve one's equilibrium on this grass, while taking leisured observations of the turmoil on the towing-path close by.

So, I strolled down quite early, intending to study the human current coming and going. I was rather too early. There were but few people about as yet. Punts and steamers and motor-boats were edging-in backward: and there were the usual clots of screeching little boy messing about the river-brink. Now and then, a racing-crew paddled (or bucketted) down to its station. But athletes occurred only in scanty sprinklings. I walked on to the end of the grass.

Suddenly, men began to swarm down in crowds. I turned back; and made for the unoccupied middle of the grass-patch. There was quite a lot of flesh on view, not (perhaps) of the quality of ten years ago, when the okhlotesacy had not yet been permitted to forget its place, and before the *Dylymyle* had made the nation a chronic self-conscious hysteric. But still it was by no means sickening; and, here and there, Nature proved that she had not entirely lost the knack of modelling shrines for character.

The gun went off; and the race began. Up came the crowd again, firing revolvers, whirling plangent wooden rattles, bellowing through mastodonic megaphones. As I had been moving slowly toward Ponti Lunghi to see the faces of the gymnasts going down, I was now sauntering back toward Iffleja to see them coming up. In a few minutes they had passed me, and were rampaging far up stream, leaving me almost alone again. I did not turn to follow, knowing jolly well what a block there would be on the towing-path above the boat-house, and the utter impossibility of crossing to the Prato della Casa di Cristo till all the boats had reached their proper barges, and the perennial puntful of performers had been tipped-over for the diversion of the leek-shaped virgins who concealed their right eyes with tubs made of the pelts of sea-green lions decorated with the residuum of a massacre of condors and albatrosses on the barge-tops.

I hope it is quite plain that I was not really seeing all these things which I describe – seeing them (I mean,) not with the two common or filmy eyes with which we keep our pipes alight and wink at auctioneers and use for not avoiding temptation, but with that third transcendental esoteric clear-seeing eye hidden in the brain which gives the only vision worth while. Of course I saw the moving show, as heaps of other people saw it, as something all-of-a-sudden fuskily epileptic in a fog, something ephemeral, essentially irreproducible, obliterated utterly, gone and done with. But I don't call that Seeing, simply because it is not Hearing.

But, when I came to the end of the grass, and stepped on to the towing-path, that third eye of mine promptly etched the last of my three pictures on my mind. Coming toward me from Iffleja and about fifty yards away, was the slight Grey Man. It was a clear vision of him, face to face, which I set myself intensely to study.

I find it nearly impossible to interpret his personality in words: it was so vivid, so serene, so supremely non-curant, so exclusively aloof and distinct from every other living thing on this orb of earth. This time, he was in white, bare-legged, bare-headed. His white jacket and socks were patterned with a fine grey line: but his shorts and his zephyr were plain. His shoes and belt were of grey suede. A dark-grey chain, slipped through the jacket-buttonhole, held a watch in the left breast pocket. His key-chain and belt-buckle were of the same dull-gleaming platinum-coloured metal. A white silk-handkerchief hid in his left sleeve, round which a towel was twisted; and the last item (taken in conjunction with the quality of his skin and the direction of his approach) led me to conceive that he had been swimming all by himself in the Cataratta di Guado-disabbia. There was not a single discord – there was not even a harsh or a feeble note, about him anywhere. He was noticeable simply and solely because he was so exquisitely simple and sole – so singularly and so pellucidly complete in himself, and apart. I suppose that he was about five feet seven inches high; and I surmised that he would strip at about ten stone. Whoever made him, evidently understood the business: but I suspect that he himself had a hand in the job.

In judging a work of this sort, I always try to avoid the vulgar mobile's error of over-estimating details. Of course, I note them, carefully, but only as the components of a unity. The well-shaped capable feet, the well-turned legs, the supple knees, the lithe reins, the generous breast, the delightful arms and shoulder and neck, the lively uniform tan of the silky skin, were (I could see in a flash) the reason, the *causa causans*, the integral elements, of this perfectly-poised personality. His gait (which, as the Preacher says, shews what a man is,) was truly marvellous in the strength and delicacy of its inevitably inerrant equilibrium. Have you ever seen one of those slim young Nipponese acrobats pacing an almost invisible wire stretched over abysmal precipices? That was the mien of the Grey Man. Only, I was sensible that he went in no danger of falling and that he could keep up eternally. *Ostreghete!* How consummately artistic it was!

[I fear that I am keeping you waiting. My excuse is the cumbrous inadequacy of language to describe what I saw while I strolled perhaps ten steps forward.]

As he came nearer and nearer, I looked for his individuality in his face. It was a pale smooth oval face, tanned to the colour of honey. It had the very high broad brow of a student and thinker, crowned by short hair of a reddish chestnut slightly silvered. The nose was daring – straight, with sensitive nostrils. The mouth also was straight – thin and firm and recondite as to the upper lip, with a tinge of gentle tenderness lurking in the slightly fuller modelling of the lower. The eyes were dark-brown and rather long, limpidly bright in the pupils, and the white of a most wonderfully pure candor. A platinum-stepped monocle belonged in the left one. The eyebrows were darker brown, authoritatively drawn across the brow from temple to temple. The chin was the chin of a jesuitical machiavellian autocrat, like (say) Caesar Augustus, cloven and fine and compact. As for the expression – I hardly know what to say. It was the most amazingly distinct and unapproachable thing which I have yet seen. There was vivid serenity, gentleness and ruthless ferocity, quiet fastidious disdain, immense knowledge of good and of evil, fancy, wistfulness, extreme sensibility and ineffable indifference, indomitable tenacity, reserve, courage, enormous and inexhaustible force, all deliberately matured and mastered and governed by grave simple self-control. In short, it was the face of a man who has attained what Aristoteles quite luminously (and quite untranslateably) calls the *Kyria Arete*.

When he was about twenty paces away from me, his hands came out of his pockets, producing a tiny tobacco-pouch and a book of huge papers; and began to roll a cigarette. They were well-formed hands, strong and brown and fine. There was a corn on the inner top joint of the right middle finger, caused (no doubt) by the habitual use of a pen. There were corns, also, on both thumb-joints, caused (no doubt) by use of the oar of a gondola – which was most strange, you know. And, finally, the hands were armed – there is no other suitable verb – armed, with four monstrous platinum-coloured rings.

He passed on my left; and so I could not quite make out the ring which was farthest away from me, on the third finger of his right hand. I only saw that it was a most massive band with a highly-projecting bezel in which a stone of sorts sparkled clearly from behind a grating. On his right first finger, however, was another rather-larger ring, the bezel of which seemed to be a section of a triangular cylinder pivoted to the points of a horse-shoe-shaped hoof. The base of the triangle clung to the finger: but its knife-edged apex projected outward; and the two visible sides appeared to be intagliate with inscriptions. It was the third and fourth fingers of the left hand which were similarly armed. This hand, of course, was quite near me; and I had no difficulty in making my inspection. The ring on the third finger had an oblong horizontal bezel quite an inch long: it was a signet, intagliate with what looked like an Eros Crucified. But the ring on the fourth finger was perhaps the most appallingly ferocious of the four. It was a plain heavy circle; and the bezel was the sharp-pointed revolving rowel of a spur.

When I say that none of these rings projected less than quarter-of-an-inch anywhere, while the prominent portions of them jutted

out a good half-inch from the fingers, you will realize what ter-
rifically trenchant weapons they really were. Given freedom, close-
quarters, physical force and skill and promptitude behind them,
and their cusped spines and sharp edges and snaggy corners and
blunt weight furnished a complete apparatus for inflicting the
whole gamut of (not necessarily mortal) mutilations, from bruising
and scratching to gashing and slicing.

And that is all.

We passed each other on the towing-path, the incarnate enigma
going toward Ponti Lunghi, while I blundered on toward the
Osteria Iside for a much-needed drink. And that is all. I don't
know who the Grey Man is, or why extreme measures are used to
secure his company, or why he punches and gashes people and
blinds them with their blood on sight, or anything at all about him
beyond what I have told you. And, on the whole, I don't think
that I want to know any more. I have received three sharp and
violently interesting impressions. I would rather not see them
worked up and coloured. They are perfectly satisfactory to me in
outline.

[*By the bye, lest I should be deemed guilty of the habit of staring, let me
hasten to explain, first, that I carefully cultivate my senses of seeing and
differentiating and selecting to help me in my mystery of painting, and,
second, that (when out to observe) I wear black glasses and keep my head
still to prevent objects from knowing how they are regarded.*]

Daughter of a Doge

[I believe the following to be as true a picture of one kind of
Venetian life and thought – a fairly representative kind too – as it
is possible to have.]

My friend, Mr Nicholas Crabbe, happened to be cruising alone
on the Calabrian coast, at the end of the year 1908, and enjoyed
the strange experience of both the great earthquake and the
seaquake from a distance just sufficiently secure. The next day,
the 29th of December, he picked, out of a totally smashed farm-
house, which had crushed and buried her uncle with her aunts
and cousins, a bruised unconscious girl of seventeen, in the tatters
of a shift and having the short hair and general appearance of a
stalwart boy, to whom he conveniently ministered on board of his
seven-ton *bragozeto*. In response to inquiry, she said that she called
herself 'Falier Ermenegilda di Bastian fu Marin': and she
proclaimed it superbly.

Now 'Marin Falier' happens to have been the Venetian name
of that Doge of Venice, who (despite his serene principate) was
decapitated as a traitor to that republic in the Year after the
Admirable Parturition of Madama Saint Mary the Virgin 1354.
And, before precipitately plunging into the bog of superior (but
fatuous) sneers concerning the progeny of traitors, visiting (like
Yahveh) the sins of the fathers upon the children, it may be wise
(O affable reader) to remember that a successful traitor is a patriot
and his treachery the purest *amor patriae*. As a matter of fact, there
was nothing particularly disgraceful about the treachery for which
Duke Marin Falier paid the price with his head. He was *disgraziato*
only in the Italian (and first) intention of the term, in that he was
so far 'out of grace and favour' with the irresponsible gods as to be
what we English call 'unfortunate'. His enemies stole a march on
him: his attempt, a simple (but bloody) one certainly, to purify
corruption, was foiled (equally bloodily) by people who preferred

their corruption unpurified. And so Duke Marin Falier of Venice lives on history's roll of infamy, because he was an unlucky victim, just as King Edward the Excellent of England will live on history's roll of fame, because He was a most adroit master of His every situation.

Ermenegilda, daughter of Bastian son of Marin son of Bastian son of Marin, called herself Falier by cognomen no doubt for the best of all reasons. A person who (in these days) actually knows the names of her father and grandfather and great-grandfather and great-great-grandfather, all in the male line, – names, too, which ascend alternately in the same antique fashion of the rungs of a ladder – may safely be suspected of possessing a notable ancestry. The Borgia, for example, the original Borgia stem which still flourishes in the descendants of that Pietrogorio Borgia of Velletri, whose fortunes were made in 1495 by the grateful Cesare, reputed son (and undoubted right-hand) of Pope Alexander the Sixth, still call themselves alternately 'Cesare Borgia' and 'Francesco Borgia'. Why? Only because those are the two most illustrious names which their family has: Cesare was the benefactor who made them, Francesco was their canonized saint.

Crabbe, then, was not violently disinclined to believe that he had scratched up from a muck-heap the daughter of a Doge, – of three Doges, to be accurate, Vital, Ordelaf, and Marin, who reigned in 1082, 1102, and 1354, respectively. The dignity of serene principate was signed in the magnificent muscular curves of neck and shoulder, as in every other physical contour, of Ermenegilda Falier. Most Venetian girls today, certainly all of pure Venetian (untainted by Tedescan) stock, have the gait of goddesses, the radiant splendour and the sweet dainty opulent tranquillity of the sun and sea of the lagoon. But evidently Mother Nature had 'tried back' in the moulding of the present person of Ermenegilda, giving her the superb saturnian almost-sexless form, the clear-souled gaze, the unwrung plucky poise of those primeval centuries, when the world – the dust, out of which the miracle of sweet flesh is made – was half-a-thousand years younger and fresher and less trodden-to-exhaustion than it is now. And he made her tell him the tale of how she, a Venetian, came into a Calabrian farm – she, the daughter (through many generations) of the 'Doge of Venice and Dalmatia and Croatia, Hypatos and Protopedro and Protosebaste of

Byzantion, Despot and Lord of a Quarter and of Half-of-a-Quarter of All the Roman Empire', with an inalienable right to wear vermilion buskins.

She was an orphan. Her father Bastian had been a gondogliere and *gastaldo* of gondoglieri at the ferry of The Trinity of Venice, as also his parents had been before him. She had not known her mother who died young. Poor little female! But, when her father was massacred (because of twopence) by the razor of one of the three *bancali* of the same ferry, a *fecia** who instantly scampered away to Argentina, in the year before the year before that in which our Patriarch, Bepi Sarto, went to do as Pope in Rome, then, a brother of her mother took her to his farm of La Tasca in Calabria which he inherited from the father of the wife to whom he had espoused himself in that province.

Nicholas was rather puzzled about this Traghetto della Trinità. He had thought that he knew all about all Venetian ferries, and it was not until long after his return to Venice that he discovered it to be the antique name – a name as antique as AD 1592 anyhow, and only used now by gondoglieri – of the well-known Traghetto della Salute.

Ermenegilda described the first nine years of her present incarnation in the parish of San Stefano in Venice, alone with Bastian her father in his little house of four rooms full of nutwood bedsteads and antique pictures large as walls, in the tiny courtyard called Malatin which lies just under the distorted bell-tower of San Stefano. Outside that parish, all the rest of Venice (excepting the Square of Saint Mark and his basilica and the markets of Rialto,) seemed to be quite unknown by her: but her acquaintance with the city's labyrinthine water-ways was of the most intimate nature.

The first thing which she had in mind succeeded on a certain Lord's Day when she was about three years old. She and Bastian were eating cherries on their doorstep; and he picked her up, laughing, and jetted her into the canal, saying, like this, that he would give her a coral-garland for her neck, if she swam the length of his gondogla, which by chance was moored thereby. She had fear: but she played the Indian and contrived to swim the course, and she gained the coral-collar, the very one which the cruel

* =*faex populi.*

25

earthquake seemingly had ravished from her throat. Crabbe says that here she flushed, flashing a quick glance at him who had found her in her swoon.

There was nothing else to say. No: she never played with other children. Bastian forbade it, saying, like this, that no one was fit to speak to his Gildo. He always called her 'Gildo' or *fio mio*, because he preferred making her his son rather than his daughter. That was why she never wore any but boy's vestments during her father's lifetime; and, in Venice, she always passed for a boy. It annoyed her and tried her mind much, when her aunts in Calabria kept her in petticoats, which hindered her and were incessantly tearing themselves. Bastian was a very sage very brave man, with nineteen banners and seventeen medals which he gained in regattas, beside the municipal prize for his gondogla. And all foresters (specially English) esteemed him. He taught her to read the prayerbook and the *Gazzettino*, and to write her name and surname, and to cook and sew as became a good gondogliere. And, naturally, (Oysters!) the polishing of the gondogla became her mansion as soon as she could row it. When? She could not clearly remember: but it must have been soon after the time when she found that she was able to swim.

She had nothing more to say: excepting, perhaps, this, which was the story of a *scherzo*, perhaps a little repugnant. Crabbe did not mind. Well then, at a proper time she took revenge of Bastian for jetting her improvisedly into the *rio*. In this way. She being small, he cut down an old oar, and scraped it very thin with a piece of broken glass, because the oars of the *poppe* were too heavy for her at that season. And he insigned her with the art and mystery of a gondogliere, at four o'clock on summer mornings, kneeling on the seat in front of her, and cursing her properly when she let her oar slip from the *forcoja*. So, one day, it succeeded that they were going like this up Canajazzo, when (suddenly) she took a temptation. Bastian was standing on the seat, for freedom in language; and there was a *barca* of sweet wood coming out of Rio Sannegrorio; and she twitched the *poppe* aside so suddenly to avoid it, that her father lost his equilibrium, and cascaded also he into Canajazzo. O Maria Vergine, but he was comic. And he banged her so uglily when he had retrieved himself, that she flung away her oar, and butted herself also her into Canajazzo, and swam back to the *traghetto*,

shouting as she went (like this,) that she would no longer row so
bisbetic a person, who had no more education than a Croat, an
Ostrogoth, or an Abyssinian. But, when she saw him mildly re-
trieving her little oar, and coming back looking very discontented
lest any of the other gondoglieri should criticize his humidity – he
being their *gastaldo* – then she ran home, and set herself to make him
a risotto for his collation of every nutriment which she could find
in the house. Now that she had grown up, she knew that that one
must have a risotto to poison a parish: for she mixed the rice with
raisins and oil and garlic and pepper and liver and cloves and red
wine and raw ham and vinegar and salt and almonds and mustard
and cheese and orange and sepia and tomatoes and whelks and
sugar and melon and fennel and all sorts of other nutriments. But
he ate every bit of it, when she very humbly brought it to his station;
and he called her a brave and a son again, he being the best of all
affectuous fathers.

And the only thing which she could remember was this. When
she was a small creature, Bastian her father used to make her accommodate herself under the poop of his gondogla all day while he
rowed the foresters, keeping herself as quiet as the good dead, and
polishing antique coins and medals to be nailed on the *porteje* of the
poppe for its embellishment. And, when (by chance) the foresters
noted her, in the inquisitive manner of the English, Bastian used
to tell them (like this) that his little son was dumb and too shy to be
spoken to: so that they would purely sniff, and leave her alone. For
he had a very proud heart, that Bastian, often telling her (like this,)
that, though the Falier were kept low and much wronged, no one in
all the Veneto had better blood: for one of the family discovered
the holy body of Saint Mark Evangelist hidden in a column of the
basilica, and was himself sepultured in the porch of it; and another
of her parents made the Pala d'Oro in Saint Mark's, and builded
the Arsenal, and made great wars in Dalmatia whence comes the
firewood and the good wine Buon Padre. Naturally one would
be proud of parents of such a type. And, when she became
larger and more expert, naturally she always rowed the poop-oar
while Bastian rowed at the prow, when rich foresters wished to
have two gondoglieri to take them far, to see the glass-makers of
Murano, or the lace-makers of Burano, or Torçelo, or Saint
Francis in the Wilds, or Saint George in the Seaweed, or the Lido,

or other islets. In this way, and with the ferrying, they gained many deniers, never less than four *franchi* a day, and sometimes as many as thirty-five or forty when they put the gilded apparatus into the *poppe* for some English *miliardario* who desiderated a gondola of luxury. But, when Bastian was massacred and dead, only ninety-one *franchi* of his were found in the bank: because they always had had the best of everything and as much as they wanted. Her uncle, who called himself Sior Polo Anafesto, chanced to be on a visit to her father at that very moment. He was a very rich benign pacific man, with twenty-four cows and an olive-grove and ninety hectares of land and innumerable congregations of turkeys, and his wife with her two old sisters in the house; and he was beloved and obsequiated by everybody. Why, when he had buried Bastian with a pomp costing some two-hundred *franchi* (which he paid out of own burse,) imagine what beneficences he did for her now speaking. He sold the gondogla for a thousand-five-hundred-and-fourteen *franchi*. A mad English dwarf living at the Tolentini bought the *ferro* of it for five-hundred *franchi*, it being very antique and as subtile as gum-elastic. And the coins which adorned the *porteje* also had much value. Also, Sior Polo sold the pictures and the bedsteads and other household stuff for a thousand-four-hundred-and-thirty-three *franchi*, which (with the ninety-one from the bank) made a total of three-thousand-and-thirty-eight *franchi*. Which immense riches he changed at the Banca Veneta for gold sterlings, each worth twenty-five *franchi*, one-hundred-and-twenty-two gold sterlings there were, most beautiful to see, beside a touch of thirteen loose *franchi* left, which she asked him to pocket as the *mancia* for his trouble. 'But he said to me (like this), "O Sacramented Jesus! O Mary Virgin! O Oysters! And also O little Oysters! And am I then the robber of an orphan?" And he took other twelve *franchi* out of his own burse, and adjoined them to the thirteen; and he made the signior of the bank give another gold sterling for them, making one-hundred-and-twenty-three gold sterlings in all. And he made these to be put in a new leathern burse as large as a baby's head, and he had it sealed with the leaden sigil of the bank, five sigils there were, so that no one would dare prepotently to open it. And, when we two were alone in the waggon of the railway which transported us to Calabria, then, my uncle Sior Polo said to me (like this,) "Gildo, this burse here of gold sterlings is yours: but no one must know of it

save we two only; and, because you are young, I shall keep it: but,
when you are fifteen years old, I shall give it to you, so that you may
buy an olive-grove in my vicinity, and espouse yourself to a wife,
and get yourself as many sons as possible before you go for a soldier
to take care of you in your old age." For he thought that I was a boy,
as indeed did all the living. So I told him how things were precisely.
And he laughed, saying (like this,) "Little Oysters!" first, and then
(like this,) "Ahi, Bastian!" Afterwards he said to me (like this,)
"A husband, then." I said (like this,) that I desiderated nothing of
that genus. And then he said (like this,) "As you will, in regard to
espousals: but I believe that your aunt Alcmena will make you a
proper girl; and it will be prudent for you to make yourself seen by
her in a petticoat at the first beginning." So, when the train stopped
one morning at a certain city called Bari, my uncle bought certain
femminile vestments there, and I put them on over my habit of
a gondogliere, rolling up my trousers over my knees, in the waggon
wherein we were journeying. And, when his wife of my uncle, my
aunt Alcmena, had seen me and had heard all things, she said to me
(like this,) "Are you, my Gilda, for gentility's sake, any better than
Maria Vergine, whom Domeniddio deigned to make feminine?"
To which there was nothing to be said.' So Gildo of Venice became
Gilda in Calabria, and a good enough girl but for her awkwardness
in the habit femminile.

'How did I pass the time at La Tasca? Like this. In the first
beginning, I boxed the farm-boy, ping-pong pang-pung, because
he dared to look at me. In consequence, none of the neighbouring
peasants would send their sons to my uncle's service, for fear of
what they called the savage turkish she who was of his family.
"It goes well," said I, even me, (like this,) to Sior Polo, "and now I
myself will be your farm-boy, being very svelt and strong, though
femminile. Isn't it true? And, when I shall have made myself
expert in the art and mystery of the farm, I will teach the same to
Archimede my young cousin." Sior,' she addressed Crabbe, 'that
one was the junior of me by two years, and most sympathetic; and
now he lies torn in half longways by the earthquake in the ruins of
La Tasca. He was brave also, but not half as strong as I am. Poor
little he!

'I said to my uncle, then, (like this,) "As a favour and for
gentility's sake and for the Love of God, buy a bark instantly; and

I and Archimede will carry the milk in it, every morning to the Bars of Melito, and every evening to Bova Marina and the Tower of Saint John of Avolo, this saving the expense of the railway." Thus, we did. I also worked in the olive-grove: for Sior Polo said that my condition ameliorated that of his olives, which became the best in that vicinity after I had taken them in hand: for no one touched the trees but me, not even with a finger-tip, not even my cousin Archimede. What more? I helped my aunt, the Siora Alcmena to do well by her babies, (I being appassionated for babies,) and to serve her very old sister who was bedridden, through a bull which broke her back when young and prevented her from espousing herself to a husband. She was purely holy, that old she; and she insigned me with the whole of the Christian Doctrine. Am I Christian? Mah! What else, Sior, when Papa Bepi Himself chrisomed me in our basilica of San Marco when He was our Patriarch and before He went to pontificate in Rome. And the other two sisters of my aunt Alcmena – also old, but not as old as the holy oldest, who was incredibly old – they taught me other clean and virtuose mysteries, as Your Sioria shall presently see. I say no more of them. I continue the history.

'Two years ago, on the first of January, being the day of my *natalizio* as well as a double festival of the first class with an octave, my uncle Sior Polo said to me (like this,) "My Gilda, this day you are grown up, being fifteen years old; and I here consign to you your proper burse containing one-hundred-and-twenty-three sterlings of gold, sealed with the five leaden sigils of the Banca Veneta." What a faithful man was that one! And I was rather frightened about these riches, having forgotten them, and not knowing what to do with them. So, I said to him (like this,) "With permission, I wish to speak with my aunt Eufemia about it:" she being the oldest. And she said to me (like this,) "My Gilda, that burse of gold sterlings is your proper portion; and you must accept it: but you may do a meritorious act if you accept it as coming from Santermenegildo, your name-saint, and on his festival, the thirteenth of April next; and so you will have three months in which to pray to him to give you good advice as to what you ought to do with your portion." Thus, then, I did. But Santermenegildo never deigned me a single word: though no doubt he would have told me something if I had been Ermenegildo instead of Ermenegilda.

And, on the thirteenth of April, which was my *onomastico*, Sior Polo
my uncle gave me the burse of one-hundred-and-twenty-three gold
sterlings; and I hid it in a hollow in an olive-tree in the very middle
of the grove, where it was quite secure, because the mere touching
of the trees was prohibited to everyone but me. And that has been
the bane of my life – that burse. I had no need of a similar mound
of gold sterlings, nor had my uncle, nor had his family of my uncle.
We were all sane: we all worked: we all gained, and were quite
contented. My uncle and my aunts and my cousins each had good
portions of their own secured to them: I had my wages of all those
years secured to me; and none of us had need of anything . . .'

Nicholas Crabbe interrupted. He, as I have mentioned, had
picked this girl out of the fragments of her ruined home and the
pieces of her slaughtered relations, taken her on board his *bragozeto*
to revive and feed and clothe her as best he could; and was sailing
eastward, hugging the coast, toward the nearest city, Bianco, where
he hoped to find some nuns, or other meritorious females, who
might be bribed to take care of her. When, though, he heard her
last words, 'And where is that burse now?' he suddenly demanded.

'Where should it be, Sior, but in the hollow olive? It was there
yesterday – I mean the day before yesterday: for I put my hand in
to taste it; and the leathern bag was so sodden soft with rain that I
could taste the gold sterlings plainly through it. Yes: now Santermenegildo has it; and I (thanks be to God) am freed from it.'

They had rounded Cape Spartivento; and were sailing north-
eastward past the semaphore station. Nicholas grimly reversed the
rudder, taking a tack to return by the way in which they had come.

'Sior, and where now?' asked Gilda, with apprehension.

'Back to La Tasca, for your portion,' grimly answered Crabbe.

Instantly she sprang on her feet. All her softness, all her sweetness,
all her exquisite persuasive gentleness of exterior had vanished.
Her mind shewed immutable, through her body as tense as a cat's.
'Sior, for charity, do the pleasure of looking the other way, while I
relinquish to you these your garments lent to me: for I will not go
back to La Tasca in this *bragozeto*.' She began to tear off the
neckerchief.

'How then will you go?'

'Sior, I will never go back to La Tasca alive.' She kicked off the
slippers.

C   31

'But your portion . . .'

'Sior, it is not mine. I said that I would take it from the saint: but he did not deign it to me. Let him keep it, then.' She untied the cord of the bath-gown at her young pulsating throat. Bare-chested, she bounded to leap on the gunwale, slipping out one scarlet shoulder and stalwart boyish arm – the other tearing the cord-knot at her waist –

'Stay firm! Mind your head! Go and shut yourself in the cabin, and weep for your numerous sins!' cried Nicholas, as the yard swang over and he steered north-eastward once more.

'Sior, *prego*,' whimpered Ermenegilda, cowed, purple, scrabbling at her coverings, and creeping away, victorious, but meek as an inheritor of the earth, all of a sudden.

Temptation

Geoffrey Lygon was busy in his attic studio one winter evening. An inspiration had come upon him, and he was modelling an *alto-rilievo*, in which he endeavoured to give expression to his conception of the angel-form which the Italians call 'bel ucel di Dio'.

The world wore a very serious aspect for him just then. For, nine years before, his conversion from high Anglicanism to the Catholic Faith, had blasted his career, deprived him of his relations and friends, and brought ruin, utter and complete, upon him. Too proud to become a hanger-on, or to submit to the degradation of amateur or professional philanthropy, he had betaken himself to London in the hope of being able to make a living there by honest work, 'which', he said, 'can stain no man's shield'. Nevertheless, though he had talent, energy, the advantage of inherited culture of cultured sires, the training and polish of Oxford and Rome, and the wider horizon of travel, he had not yet contrived to make his footing good or to earn more than the barest pittance for his needs. An artist by temperament, he lacked *technique*, the conventional *technique* of the schools, or the blatant impertinence of nineteenth-century black and white work. But among two widely-divided classes, the *cognoscenti* and the utterly-uncultured, he met with appreciation. Still, this did not help his pocket, for the *cognoscenti* and the utterly-uncultured are poor; and he gladly refused to degrade his art into a money-grubbing business. 'If people like what I do, they are welcome to buy it. If not, so much the worse for them, not for me, for I can always sweep a crossing in Carlyle Place.' But, at rare intervals, people did buy; and on this and occasional articles in the magazines he managed to just live and no more. Now, though, he was feeling the effect of many long months of solitude and semi-starvation which made him incapable of writing acceptable 'copy' for his editors, while the want of materials prevented him from going on with his pictures.

He had modelled the young figure of his 'bird of God' poised in space upon spreading pinions, with a sensuous pleasure in the promise of the lovely proportions and contours of youth, when a knock at the door and the entrance of his barrister-acquaintance, Deighton, aroused him from the inspection of his work.

'I have brought a lady to see you,' said Deighton, who was a notorious misogynist.

Lygon went to the landing to assist this unexpected visitor up the Jacob's ladder of this staircase, and when the introductions had been performed, and the callers had seated themselves, the lady plunged without delay into the following statement, to which Lygon, who stood wiping the wet clay from his hands, listened with the astonishment of entire unpreparedness. Mrs Maltravers gabbled like a turned-on tap of water.

'I went to Mr Deighton this afternoon to ask him to recommend a gentleman to act as tutor to the dear boy who is my ward, and he could think of no one more suitable than yourself. Johnnie is the son of an English father who is dead, and an Italian mother of whom we do not speak. He is the most delightful and beautiful creature, winning in manner, a splendid athlete though he is only fifteen, and very clever. But there is insanity in his family, which has already shown itself in his sister who is at a school in Hampshire, from which I have undertaken to remove her at the notice of a telegram in the event of her breaking out. Johnnie, however, has given no sign of it, except, perhaps, in the cat-like activity, with which he leaps and climbs the most impossible places. He is at a medical school at Windsor, kept by the celebrated Dr and Mrs Thompson, where his health is most carefully looked after. I have an arrangement with these people and the Court of Chancery, by which I appoint a gentleman to be with Johnnie as companion in his games and tutor for his lessons. The appointments of the School are magnificent, and you would be made most comfortable; medical care free of charge, and plenty of spare time for yourself while Johnnie is at his classes. The salary is only £40 a year, but that is all pocket money, you see. I do hope you accept the post.'

Lygon was rather taken aback by this point-blank offer. On the spur of the moment it looked like a very happy deliverance from the sordidness of his life, but at the same time he asked himself whether he thought he was a fit person to undertake the somewhat serious

34

responsibilities of the office; and he suggested that he had better go and see the place and the boy before making any decision.

Mrs Maltravers agreed to arrange this; and, having settled upon the ensuing Saturday for the visit, she departed, reiterating her desire that Lygon should accept, and her assurances that the position was exactly suited to him.

Saturday morning came, bringing with it a note from Mrs Thompson asking Lygon to call upon her, and Mrs Maltravers in person, who sat in the studio all the morning saying, over and over again, all that she had said at her previous visit.

About mid-day she had tired her tongue out, and Lygon was permitted to leave for his inspection [of the] medical school at Windsor.

He returned to town the same evening; and, on his way home, he called upon Mrs Maltravers, and announced that, after considering the matter, he was obliged to say that he was not strong enough to undertake the duties of tutor to Johnnie Palmer.

'Was ever anything more disappointing in the world?' cried Mrs Maltravers. 'And we had set our hearts upon you, Mr Lygon! I know you are not strong, – just now, – Mr Deighton told us all about you, – but you could be nursed up at Windsor, you know.' And for an hour she went over the same tale.

Lygon was sorely tempted to risk it. He knew what he knew, and why he had decided to refuse the post. Still, he thought, perhaps he might be hypersensitive; and things would turn out well despite his gloomy forebodings. Yes, the temptation was very strong, but in the end he resolved to adhere to his refusal, and risk the rest.

On the Monday after, Mrs Maltravers sent for Lygon, and informed him that she had been mystified beyond measure; for, after he had refused the post on Saturday, she had a note from the proprietress of the medical school refusing him: and she begged Lygon to make a clean breast of all that had happened at Windsor to bring about such a confusion.

Lygon hated a mystery; and feeling that nothing in the world was really worth making a secret of, replied, openly and frankly, that he had seen the place and the boy, and had heard Mrs Thompson's description of the vacant post, and, finding that it differed entirely from that of Mrs Maltravers in certain particulars, which he unreservedly stated, he had been assured of its being a baseness on his part to accept responsibilities which he could not fulfil. But when he began to go into details, and had spoken for about two minutes, Mrs Maltravers interrupted him with a scream.

'But that is against the order of the Court! She cannot do that! She tried to do so before but the Court of Chancery made an order to restrain her.'

Lygon insisted that things were exactly as he had stated; and then Mrs Maltravers asked if he would be willing to write down what he had said. He replied that it would give him much pleasure to do so, and that if Mrs Thompson desired to refute his statements he was prepared to fortify them with an affidavit before the Court of Chancery, to whom, he supposed, they would be submitted.

Then he went and told Deighton.

'But, my dear chap,' said the barrister, 'it's a mad-house you're describing!'

'Quite so,' rejoined Lygon, 'it is a mad-house. Mad-house stares you in the face there, and I'm not going to live in one, even as an official, in my state of health. Why, it would make me dotty at once. And as for the unfortunate boy, he's as sane as you are; and, I understand, has been begging his guardian to take him away because he's afraid of going silly himself. It's a regular job, and I shall make my statement to Mrs Maltravers as forcible as I know how, even if I have to defend a libel action.'

Before the end of the week, Lygon had written his impressions to Mrs Maltravers and this is what he said:

Mrs Thompson informed me that the Tutor would rank as an Officer of the Asylum. The duties of an Officer of the Asylum were defined in two books, viz. in a book entitled *Rules for Officers* and in a book entitled *Rules for Attendants*. Mrs Thompson led me to understand that I would have to subscribe to these Rules and to be bound by them. I noticed therein that an officer was not allowed to carry a walking-stick when he was in attendance on his patient; that he was also forbidden to read a book, or even peruse a private letter while on duty. I asked Mrs Thompson to be allowed a copy of the rules, but she refused.

Mrs Thompson said that Johnnie Palmer's Tutor must be prepared to give the whole of his time to her as an Officer of the Asylum. He was to keep constant watch upon Johnnie Palmer except at such times when he was employed in teaching the junior inmates of her establishment.

The Tutor must be prepared not to smoke in the presence of the pupils, never on the premises except in the masters' room between 9.30 and 10.30 p.m.; which was a matter of impossibility for Johnnie Palmer's Tutor, because he had to be in attendance upon his charge at that time. I listened carefully to all that Mrs Thompson had to say, and tried to obtain all the information which I could about the work of the Tutor, without expressing any opinion of my own, and in fact saying as little as possible.

I was taken over the establishment by the matron. I saw two houses, called respectively North House and South House. The matron explained that North House, where Mrs Thompson lived, was divided into two asylums visited by the Lunacy Commissioners. South House is separated from North House by a winding path. These two places are not more than five minutes' walk apart. At South House I saw a dining room, a drawing room, a schoolroom, and the room where the masters are suffered to smoke between 9.30 and 10.30 p.m. I was also shown the bedroom to be occupied by Johnnie Palmer and the Tutor. I noticed two small wooden beds, a chest of drawers, washstand and dressing-table. There were also several prayer-books and a photograph of Johnnie Palmer; but there was no writing-table for the use of Johnnie Palmer or the Tutor, or any other conveniences for the purpose of making the room suitable as a sitting room. It struck me that it would not have been wholesome for two people, one of them being a delicate and growing lad, to live in that room, if it were intended to be a sitting room as well as a bedroom. Another thing that struck me was that there was no privacy in the room, and that the Tutor would have to make his toilet, without reserve, in the presence of the boy, a thing which is unheard of at all respectable Catholic schools, and calculated to shock the modesty of any decent man or boy.

I saw Johnnie Palmer taking exercise in an iron shed with the other inmates, and the matron stated that all the boys, with the exception of Johnnie Palmer, were 'not right'.

I was unfavourably impressed. It was quite evident that no Tutor of Mrs Maltravers' nomination would be acceptable to Mrs Thompson. I disliked the system of espionage which appeared to be the custom of the place. I am convinced that it is a very unfit place for Johnnie Palmer to live in; as all, or the greater part at least, of his companions are admitted to be of unsound mind.

I formed such a strong opinion, that, on my return from Windsor, I went immediately to Mrs Maltravers, and declined the post, on the ground that the state of my health would prevent me from performing the duties of Tutor to Johnnie Palmer.

As you must be able to see, I have all along been most unwilling to say anything against Mrs Thompson. It is contrary to my own interest to do so; but, at your express desire, I have merely given you my opinion, and I have tried to be as moderate as is consistent with frankness.

For a few days, Lygon had peace. He felt glad that he had been able to give to Mrs Maltravers his unbiased opinion of the place in which her ward was living; and, if need be, he was ready to have his evidence submitted to the Court of Chancery. But, as events turned out, this was not necessary. Mrs Thompson had the opportunity of reading what he had said, and she wrote some very nasty letters about him to Mrs Maltravers. These were laid before Mr Deighton the barrister who advised Mrs Maltravers, and he pointed out that Mrs Thompson had not been able to traverse a single statement of Lygon's, and that all she had to say simply amounted to the ravings of an angry woman. He made use of the *clichés*, 'Hell knows no fury like a woman scorned', and '*spretae iniuria formae*', with much effect. Then two or three interviews took place between the two ladies, and Mrs Maltravers gave Lygon to understand that some very stormy scenes were enacted. But Lygon observed, although as he had said it was no concern of his, that Johnnie Palmer remained in the lunatic asylum; and that a youth was found, by Mrs Maltravers, to take the tutorship, and to be denounced a fortnight later, by Mrs Thompson, as having been guilty of spelling 'grammar' with an 'e'.

But, as time went on, Lygon found that his own mind was almost entirely occupied by the matter. And the thought grew with him that he ought to do something, he could not see plainly what that something was, to save this unhappy child from losing his senses; for he had settled as much as this with himself, that, if Johnnie Palmer spent the most impressionable years of his life with mad people, the wit of man or fiend could devise no surer forcing-house for the development of the germ of insanity which, Mrs Maltravers had confessed, was in his family.

When, then, he saw his way clearly, he acted with promptitude, and paid a visit to Johnnie Palmer's guardian. He found her, clad in a dimity petticoat and a sealskin jacket, sitting on the stairs, cursing the painters who were decorating her staircase. Her face was hideously dirty; and a habit of wiping her nose with an upward movement of the palm of her hand had given to the under side of that organ a jet-black polish. And she had potatoes on her heels. She received Lygon with *empressement*, and poured forth her intentions of having her ceilings painted blue with raised golden stars, and a maiolica on the landing in a fish-frame with cherubs' heads. He listened, with deference, to her ramblings, until she had given him the whole history of her travels in Arabia, and the lamps she had bought from mosques there; and, as soon as he was able to get a word in edgeways, he began to enquire about the ward. This was evidently an unpleasant subject, and Mrs Maltravers was not pleased when he repeated his opinion that she was taking the shortest road to driving the boy mad, by confining him in a lunatic asylum.

'But surely I am to be persecuted till I'm crazy over it,' she screamed; 'I know there is danger, but Mrs Thompson has promised me to have every precaution taken; and *I am afraid to offend her.*'

'My dear Mrs Maltravers,' Lygon replied, 'what can there be to make you afraid of Mrs Thompson? She is nothing to *you* but the keeper of an asylum. You pay her, or rather the Court pays her, for everything, and you can be under no possible obligation to her. Your duty is to your ward; and, though I am a comparative stranger to you, I must in common honesty tell you that you are quite wrong in your treatment of him. I am sure that there are hundreds of places in England where the boy could be properly taken care of, and where he could get the education and companionship of lads of his own rank, which would build up his mental and physical constitution, and give him a chance of a sane and healthy manhood. He has a right to this, an indefeasible right; and it is my firm conviction that, if you deprive him of this right, you will do him the greatest injustice. Why do you not consult the Court about it? I am sure I do not want to interfere with what is not my concern; but I cannot look on, and watch this charming boy drifting towards madness like this, without anyone to stand up for him and take his part.'

When it came to that, Mrs Maltravers burst into tears. She was worried out of her life, she said; her house had been turned topsy-turvy by the decorators for 18 months, all the bedroom furniture was piled up in the bathroom, and here was Mr Maltravers swearing he would go up the Nile for the winter. That meant £100 a month; and how, in the name of goodness, was she to be able to afford gold stars made in Germany for her ceilings, and fish frames for her maiolica, at this rate. And now she was being pulled in pieces by Mrs Thompson on the one side, and her duty to her ward, which she knew very well without anyone to tell her, on the other. Was Mr Lygon aware that she had promised to remove Johnnie Palmer's sister from her convent at a moment's notice if she became violent; and she had already given every indication that she was likely to go frantic at any minute? And to whom in the world could she consign her but to Mrs Thompson? Mrs Thompson had agreed to receive the girl as a lunatic at any hour of the day or night; and Mrs Maltravers was afraid that, if she made a fuss about Johnnie, this offer of Mrs Thompson's would be withdrawn.

Then Geoffrey Lygon became indignant, and tried to show the frightened woman how ridiculous was the dilemma upon which she was impaling herself.

'In plain language,' he said, 'you are going to sacrifice the reason of the brother, in order to ensure yourself against the temporary inconvenience which may, and it is only *may*, be caused you in the event of the sister going mad. Can't you see that the ruin of the boy is certain, if you let the present state of things go on, but that the ruin of the girl is only a matter of conjecture? Really, Mrs Maltravers, you are either a very foolish or a very wicked woman! Think, you are the guardian of these children, and you are bound, by every law of conscience and honour, to act for their welfare, even at a sacrifice to yourself. If you don't choose to be inconvenienced, go to the Court of Chancery and get your guardianship annulled. But I warn you, that if you do not go, I shall. It is not my affair, I acknowledge, I have simply come across this boy in my road through life, and I can see that he is being shamefully abused. I ask you, who are responsible for him, to save him; but, if you refuse, I shall consider it my duty to stand by him in his need. For it *is* a man's duty to stand by any helpless child who has no natural relation to do him a kindness.'

And the honest fervour of Lygon's manner forced itself into the unstable woman's heart, and she promised to do what he proposed, and take the advice of the Court of Chancery as to the best means of securing Johnnie Palmer's welfare.

Some weeks passed by, during which Geoffrey heard no more of the case.

His own predicament was desperate; for, with the months of insufficient food which he had gone through, his brain absolutely refused to work at anything requiring consecutive thought. His few remaining goods and chattels went, one after another, to the pawn-shop; and then his clothes followed. Two false friends, to whom he had lent his last £40, a year before, when they were in straits, refused to pay him.

'You can County-court us,' they said, 'and even then we needn't pay.'

At last he had nothing but the clothes he wore, and these were direfully shabby; he earned a scone or two and a cup of tea a day, by haunting press agencies and picking up odds and ends of work. Fleet Street was like hell to him: the rush, the clamour, the petti-fogging sententiousness, the hypocrisy, the dishonourable dealings, were like sword-thrusts to his sensitive soul.

'Lord God,' he prayed, 'kill me if You will, but let me die with clean hands, and with my chrisom-robe as white and stainless as my forefathers' shield.'

One day he had been to gather information at an inquest; and, on returning to the Press Agency which had engaged him for the job at eighteen pence, he was writing out twenty copies of the usual *flimsy* for transmission to the big Dailies, when another uneasy devil, like himself, came in.

'Are you there, Lygon?' he asked. Then, addressing someone on the stairs, 'Yes, sir, he is in. Will you walk this way?' A little man with a fair moustache entered.

'Mr Lygon, I believe?' said he. 'Very pleased to make your acquaintance. Can I have a few minutes' conversation with you?'

'In half a moment,' Lygon replied; concluding his *flimsy* – much sympathy was expressed with the parents of the deceased who was a bright and winning girl – 'There you are, Mayborn, put those in envelopes and send them round the morning list. Now sir,' turning to the stranger, 'I am at your service.'

Poor Geoffrey's heart was beating a little faster, for he smelt an Editor, a big Editor, and, more than that, an Editor who had taken off his hat and come to ask a favour.

'If you are a smoker, Mr Lygon,' said the Editor, 'I think you will find it worth while to try one of these.' And he held out a gold cigar-case. Geoffrey chose a weed, cut the fish-tail, and lighted up. He had been considered a judge of Cabañas at Oxford; and the first whiff was bliss, after a year of Mackrell and Goldstein's threepenny shag.

'I suppose you have seen the morning papers?' his visitor continued. 'No? Well, I have some cuttings which you might care to look over.'

He handed them to Lygon, who could not prevent himself from starting at some names, underlined, which immediately caught his eye.

'You remember that last Whitechapel murder, Mr Lygon? And that the murderer had succeeded in baffling the police? Yes? Well, you will see from these cuttings that they arrested him this morning upon his own confession, and that he turns out to be a mad boy who had escaped from a lunatic asylum.'

Lygon listened like one in a dream, and pored over the cuttings. The Editor laid a hand on his shoulder and said: 'Now, Mr Lygon, to be quite plain with you, I represent the *Diurnal Snort*; and it has come to my knowledge that you possess exclusive information about a child, who, though perfectly sane, is confined in that very asylum, consorting with dangerous maniacs. If you will let me have that information, I am willing to deal very liberally with you, and we might even create a post for you on our permanent staff, if you cared to join us. No, don't make your mind up in a hurry, Mr Lygon. This is a most important thing, you know.'

Geoffrey winced under the pressure of his hand.

'I'm afraid it can't be done, sir,' he said simply.

'But why not?' persisted the Editor. 'You must not stand in your own light, Mr Lygon.'

'Oh, I don't want to stand in my own light,' said Geoffrey, 'but I cannot do what you wish.'

'Now look here, Mr Lygon,' rejoined the Editor, 'you come along and have a bit of lunch with me, and we'll talk the matter over. I know you're the soul of honour and all that, and I'm sure I shall be able to persuade you that even in Fleet Street we're not so black as you paint us. I read your article on "Press Ethics" in the *Carlton Gazette*, and a very smart bit of writing it was. In fact I said at the time that we must get hold of the writer for the *Diurnal Snort*. Now

I'll just run across the road for a minute and send a telegram; and, by the time you've put your *flimsies* away, I'll come and fetch you.' And he was gone.

Geoffrey's head was whirling round and round. He went downstairs like one in a dream, and was pushed gently into a private hansom by his Editor.

'Look here, sir,' said Geoffrey, 'I cannot come with you and eat your luncheon on false pretences, so you really had better drop me before we go any further.'

They whisked along the Strand.

'I can't give you a reason, because your business was so unexpected that it has sent my wits a wool-gathering; but, you know, I can't give you what you want. Anything else I should be very happy to do. Perhaps you will let me send you some copy now and then. I have lots by me.'

'Copy,' cried the Editor, 'why my dear Mr Lygon, we shall be delighted to have as much as you can send us. And, as for the other matter, we shall meet my proprietor at lunch; and I'm sure the two of us will be able to convince you that you will only be doing an act of justice by placing the papers in our hands. Fleet Street has a way, you know, of ferretting out facts; I needn't tell you how we came by our information, but we know that you have evidence of a very damning character against this lunatic asylum, we know that it was drawn up for you by counsel in the form of an affidavit, and we want the draft. You see, if we can lay the facts of the case before the public, and establish our contention that a sane boy is being imprisoned, and contaminated, by the companionship of homicidal maniacs like this murderer, we shall obtain an excellent boom for the *Snort* and do a kindness to the boy at the same time.'

The rest is lacking

Arrested as a Spy

While I was cleaning my front doorsteps this morning and planning the form of this experience, – doorsteps on the Grand Canal get covered with seaweed, and slippery, in three days, during the hot summers; and no Venetian (my landlord Count Luigi Sbrojavacca had to send to ask me how I did it) can clean them as lustrously and as thoroughly as I do, with old brooms and chloride of lime, every day when I'm at home – it was borne in upon me most forcibly, that, to avoid any possible stupid misunderstanding or unpleasantness, I had better at this stage of the records of my Venetian experiences, make no more ado, divest myself of all disguises and begin at once abruptly by stating, once for all, and quite frankly, and as emphatically as I know how to state it, that I (not to put too fine a point upon it) *love the Venetians with all my heart and soul.* I do hope to Goodness that's quite unmistakeably clear. The fact is, a Venetian of Carthaginian origin, πάσχουσι δὲ τοῦτο δι' ἀπαιδευσίαν, whom I lately have had occasion to criticise, has been whimpering that I am accustomed to *sperlare*, i.e. to 'dispeak' or to speak against the Italians; and of course nothing could be more entirely and gratuitously erroneous. I should never dream of doing such a silly thing. To begin with, I don't know a dozen real Italians, and I'm not such a fool as to generalize on a mere dozen of particulars. It's like this. Massimo d'Azeglio said: *Ora che è fatta l'Italia, bisogna fare gli Italiani.* (Now that we have made Italy, we must make the Italians.) And the only inhabitants of this peninsula, whom I really have studied somewhat attentively for the last five years, (besides the English and Scotch μετοίκοι), are the Teutonic-Mongol-Slavic-Asiatic-Greco-Hebrew-Arabic-Latin-Italiot congeries who (at present) call themselves and are called Venetians. These, I love. They are, I believe, in process of conversion into Italians as Massimo d'Azeglio designed. They seem to me to be in a rather unfinished (I dare not say 'unbaked') stage at present: but that perhaps is due to the fact that they have never enjoyed the blessed discipline of the Feudal

44

System, and (so) present a more complacent and banausic and a less malleable material than the Tuscans or the Romans or the Piemontesi etc. One of their own wonderfully perspicacious critics says that, in judging them, it must never be forgotten that they are *un popolo granbambino*, i.e. 'a big-baby people', i.e. that they are huge (and therefore very insistently notable,) and, also, very very very very young. Anyhow, – let no one mistake me – I love the Venetians, as I said. *Amoris hoc argumentum, non malignitatis.* And, therefore, following the highest and the best example, I, in surest proof of my love, freely criticize (chastise) them. The little dears! *Quem amat Dñs castigat.*

Further, let it be clearly understood that I speak solely of the Venetians whom I know. I am perfectly aware that there are many who are quite different. There must be – it stands to reason that there must be: – otherwise, Venice would have been blotted out, in the usual course of things, like the Cities of the Plain, ages ago. The misfortune is that so far I have never met those other people Περὶ μὲν οὖν τῶν ἄλλων ἔστω τις ἕτερος λόγος.

Well then: it was late in the autumn of 1909 and a very lovely morning indeed. I was quite alone. My lodging on the open landing of a staircase in Palazzo Mocenigo-Corner seemed repulsive. One friend in England who had stolen the MSS of two of my books, was refusing to give them up unless I paid him £625 or let him publish them under his own name, and another was damning me because I wouldn't write a novel about a saint for him to sign. *Si Deus benignus, ut quid sacerdos Euis malignus?* I was in great misery, and very heartsick. *Paralus miles arma non habui.* I was made with Job to possess months of vanity and nights of weariness were appointed to me. And the dirty streets of Venice full of *nani, gobbi, zoppi*, i.e. dwarves, humpbacks, cripples, and the curious ladies and gentlemen who grow gigantic warts, or large long hairy turkey-tufts out of unexpected sites on their cheeks, throats, and brows, (of which human phenomena there seem to be more in Venice than in any other city known to me) bored me to extinction. I thought that a day on the lagoon in the lovely perfect solitude of wide horizons, with the sea and the sky for my sole companions, would clean me up and invigorate me. *Hoc amo quod possum, qualibet, ire via.* So I went down to the Bucintoro Rowing Club (of which I was then a member) with a packet of bread and cheese and an onion and a flask of water; and got out the puparin with the aid of Fausto Levi. He was rather attentive that day; and, by the mercy of the gods, I was by chance in a position to tip him rather heavily. The puparin is a variant of the gondogla, a slim light bark about 8–9 yards long, without the gondogla *ferro* at prow, and with the poop formed like a bird's tail folded, but pertly tilted upward like that of a merle at moments. You stand balancing on the poop to row it in the mode Venetian. I didn't overload the bark, not being then an expert oarsman, and desiring to row as lightly as possible. I wore my Union Jack at the prow – the same which, some time afterwards, I, delirious in pneumonia, insisted on using as a nouselling cloth when they gave me the Viaticum. I took also a spare oar, a burberry, the usual lantern for night use, and my two charts of the lagoon, with some bits of rope for tying up and very little (if anything else). And I rowed across the Basin of St Mark and by St George the Great into the Canal of La Grazia which leads southward. The current was in my favour; and the weather delicious. I had no particular plan, excepting to take an old Tauchnitz novel to one of the doctors at the Female Madhouse on the island of San Clemente, about a mile out, and then just to dawdle about, sucking up tenacity, wile and endurance of evil from my exquisite surroundings.

I shall always believe that the more or less pleasant adventures of that day and night were the due punishment of my crime against courtesy at San Clemente. One always does get back precisely what one gives. I didn't make any long stay with the doctor: not being in a mood for polite conversation, but merely left the book, told him that I distinctly revered and obsequiated him and came away. But, down at their landing stage, where I had tied up the puparin, there was a very pleasing young friar, a real Franciscan, (none of your bearded Capuchins,) nicely tonsured and sandalled all complete, who appeared to have been ministering to some maniac. He had the air of being marooned there, for no bark was waiting to take him away, and the hourly steamboat was nowhere in sight; and he asked me pleasantly if I by chance was going back to Venice. Of course I ought to have jumped at the opportunity of doing a kindness to the clergy, merely because one and all of them all my life long so far, have simply played Old Gooseberry with me, and you never ought to do as you are done by, but quite the contrary.

However, thanks to Bobugo, who tried to bully me by sending me his benediction through a freemason, instead of frankly blessing me who cursed him for his infernal cheek, had so infuriated me that I wasn't taking any clergyman that morning, thank you. I told the friar that I wasn't going back, when I might just as well have gone back with him for passenger, and perhaps have made the acquaintance of a decent priest for a change. And I rowed coldly away in the other direction. Hence, indubitably, what followed.

The broad and deep canal of Santo Spirito, along which I rowed or drifted pensively, was most soothingly empty and tranquil. When, far away in the distance, the midday gunfire of Venice called my attention back to mundane things, I tied up to the cluster of piles on the left where the fishermen's little shrine is, to eat my bread and cheese, and to doze in the warm sunshine afterward. And, while I slept, The Authorities began getting ready my punishment for me.

Perfectly stormy storms get up on this lagoon in about ten minutes. *Ubicumque dulce est, ibi et acidum invenies.* I woke up to find one on top of me and no shelter nearer than Malamocco. It's true that there was the island of Poveglia about midway on my right, with its houses and its campanile: but, somehow, it didn't strike me as interesting. It's true also that I, being made of neither sugar nor salt, rather revel than otherwise in being well-rained on. Eels, they say, get used to skinning; and I suppose I'm used to being battered about. Anyhow I ought to be. But there was the puparin to think of. It wasn't mine: for I'd made a present of it to the Rowing Club. And a puparin, which is an open bark, soon fills up with rain-water, and is then a nasty craft to manage even if she doesn't decide to settle down gunwale-deep and lollop solemnly over flat bottom upward. So I rowed ahead like forty furies.

The storm of wind and hail came down; and churned the sea up choppily but I got into Malamocco drenched to the skin and not more water in the puparin than sufficed to float the floor-boards. And, having tied up to the wooden pier, I unloaded everything ashore and took to baling with the wooden shovel which lives under every prow. A fat and sinful skinful of handsome young Bacchus observed me. The rain ceased and half-a-dozen males dawdled down and observed me and my paraphernalia too – a soldier or two, a ticket-collector or two, and some small fisher boy.

As my charts were sodden, they obligingly spread them out to dry, and observed them also with delightfully naive curiosity. As none but males were visible, I stripped myself naked and put on my dry burberry, squeezing out my wet clothes and hanging them on the rails. It was a queer costume, not exactly ugly, but one's legs emerging from a burberry do look astonishingly leggy and long and sudden. However, my companions were vested verisimilarly and showed no abnormal stupefaction.

It began to rain steadily again. I got half the puparin under the little pier and piled my goods up in it under cover; and strolled into the pub at the pier-end to stir the blood with a little beaker of wine while waiting for more clement weather. Here also everyone else (excepting the ladies) wore waterproofs and bare skins. Every twenty minutes, or so, I skipped to the pier-end and baled out the bark, till three o'clock when there came a glimpse of sunshine and (I regretted to see) a freshening of the already sufficient north-wind. But I got my ship dry (comparatively) for about the ninth time, and began to think about returning to Venice: when, lo, my spare oar was missing. Now, as the Bacchus youth had been the last person near when I had previously baled the puparin, I coursed back to the pub, where that suspect had been distended dozing at my departure. His bench was empty. I pranced into the interior; and (I don't know why) into the back yard in the rear, to the amazement of everybody. And there was my snapper-up of unconsidered trifles, carefully placing my oar under his shed. 'What doest dear thou with that my oar?' I sweetly asked. 'Sior, with permission, I was putting it in security from the rain, don't you know.' I took it away from him. 'Sior, at least regale me with a tip, to recompense me, for gentility's sake.' I told him where he could go. *Nemo nostrum non peccut: homines sumus non dii.*

It will be better to be brief about the punishment for my bad-temper to the friar at San Clemente, which began in earnest immediately when I set off on my five-mile row-back at three-thirty from Malamocco. It began with a strong tide against me, which only let me reach Poveglia – less than a mile – at five-thirty. I seemed to be the only soul alive on all the vast grey grisly lagoon, excepting a fisherman, who was preparing to rush his sandolo back to Malamocco, having roared prophecies of hideous storms to me when I refused his offer to take me to Venice for L.30. His prophecies were verified at once. I struggled on from Poveglia, in the teeth of a deluge of rain, against the current, and against the furious north wind, which not only refused to let me advance across the open, but drove me violently back, at seven, breaking my prow on a pile and filling me to within four inches of the brim with seawater. There was nothing to do but to refuge on the island, at least till I had baled out the bark. I saw a little canal which ran into it on the south side and contrived to enter and to reach a stone quay whereon were inhabited houses, with open doors, and voices heard within. I said 'Oh!' loud. Non-commissioned-officer sort of persons coursed wildly out of doors shrieking the Venetian equivalent for 'Avaunt, intruding thou!' I explained and demonstrated my predicament. Would they, for gentility's sake, let me land, bale out, and rest for half an hour? Ah, how desolated and displeased they were: but the island of Poveglia was a fort, oh but *fortissimo*, and ingress was prohibited, oh but *proibitissimo*, in any conceivable circumstances whatever. I invited them to view my water-logged bark, the fierce storm, the fast growing night, and to consider the possibility of my being drowned outside. They implored me not to think of anything so fastidious. If I would only row for ten minutes up the canal across the lagoon to my right – the proper Canale di Poveglia, don't you know – I should find there a piroga of the dazio whose officials would rescue me and refuge me and lavish every attention. So I wabbled out of Poveglia, into the tempest and the darkness of the open lagoon again.

Do you see what I meant by my preliminary observations about a *popolo granbambino*, O most affable reader? Isn't it characteristic of a big-baby people to be snuffy about letting anyone else play with its toys? Isn't it? I don't want anyone's toys – I mean forts. Even if they personally conducted me over their forts, and elaborately let me into all the secrets of their forts, I should understand not a single thing about their forts. I'm not that sort of capable person, and I'm not interested. Besides, I have other things to think about. But, even if I did know all and everything about their forts, I love the Venetians far too dearly – yes, I really do love them: but I think it fair to say also that I love myself far too dearly as well – to play them the nasty trick, and, in fact, to dirty my own none too clean hands, selling them to their dear allies, Germany, Austria, Hungary. This, however, they entirely fail to realize – as you shall shortly see.

49

I rowed out into the tempest and the darkness in the indicated
direction, walking entirely by faith, for no sight was possible in that
raging pitch-black night. It was absolutely necessary to keep on
rowing hard, or I certainly should have been rolled over and over
if the wind and the waves had been free to wreak their will on a
derelict. And at nine o'clock I reached the ten minutes' distant
piroga of the dazio, one of those noah's ark barges which, moored
in all the main waterways, intercept smugglers attempting to
introduce food etc to the city. The sailors tied up my puparin,
lightened her of my goods, and set to work to mend her nose and
bale her out. But I, the moment I touched the deck of the piroga,
lay down there and fell fast asleep. I suppose I must have been
slightly tired. Anyhow my memory is a blank till a little after mid-
night, when I was gently awakened and invited to come into the
cabin to speak to a gentleman. Someone had covered me up with
thick blankets as I slept on the open deck. The storms had passed,
and the moon shone brightly over a sobbing sea like a beaten
woman after rages. I felt as fit as a fiddle, and as much-contriving
much-enduring as ever.

The gentleman in the cabin was three gentlemen, all extremely
polite and affable and very much interested. No one seemed inclined
to take any liberties with me such as I should be obliged to resent.
Neve me impedias neve longius persequarius. They just asked quite
intelligent questions and wrote down my frank answers, my dead
Father's name, my Mother's maiden name, my age, profession,
and so on. And, if I would be so genteel, they said, as to accompany
them to the Lido, they would accommodate me with a bed for the
night. They had come in their own sandolo with two rowers; one
of them would accompany me in my puparin rowed by one of
their rowers, and the others would return as they came. So we set
forth in a procession of two barks passing the south end of Poveglia
and tending north-eastward by the Canale del Lazaretto. My
companion was talkative but quite pleasant; and I, who have
nothing to hide, thoroughly enjoy talking about myself and my
various contrivances and endurances – ὡς δ'οἱ πολλοὶ οὐ χρή.
It came out (one might almost say) naturally – as I keep on telling
these darlings, I didn't make my first retreat with the Jesuits, and I
haven't exhaustively studied Niccolò Machiavelli for nothing –
that my conductors were carabinieri in plain clothes and our

destination their barracks at Saint Mary Elizabeth of the Lido. 'Then I suppose I may consider myself under arrest,' I said dulcetly. O Castor and Pollux, nonò, also by Bacchus nononò nossiornò but nò! O Maryvirgin, no, we would not adopt any so brutal word as 'arrest' in regard to me. But, having heard by telephone, from Malamocco, and from Poveglia and from the piroga of the dazio that a shipwrecked foreigner was wandering about the lagoon, it became their (the carabinieri's) duty to see that he was properly treated. Hence the offer of a night's lodging; and, in the morning, I might (if I pleased) describe my experiences, and my charts, to their lieutenant. *Va benong*. Meanwhile, as the night air was chilly and my clothes very damp, I would (with permission) row my spare oar. My conductor was much shocked at the sight of my bare arms when I took off my jacket: I should catch cold in a mere zephyr, he said. But I made him admit that the English were very hard, and *molto molto resistente*, and laughingly rowed my goaler to my prison. There are prisons and prisons. Mine wasn't half bad, and my wardens certainly were delightful. They shewed me quite a decent room with two beds. Would I mind if one of them slept in the bed which I might not deign to accept for myself? Not a bit: it would be a joy to me. [To speak seriously, a carabiniere asleep is about as rare a thing as one can very well hope to see, O most affable reader.] Was I hungry? Mariavergine but how hungry I was, at that hour, half past two in the morning, not having eaten anything since my bread and cheese and onion of the previous midday. They coursed about the barracks: but the only thing to be found was a vase of plums preserved in grapeseed whiskey which they had robbed from their lieutenant's private cupboard. So I and two carabinieri sat on the bedsides chatting and devouring stolen property. After which, it's needless to say that I slept the sleep of quite the most just.

At seven, I woke, and went across to the bed of my snoring gaoler. 'Rouse thee, O Fair Male,' I said, shaking his shoulder, 'and come and observe me taking my morning bath in the lagoon off your landing-stage.' We went downstairs and I slipped into the sun-kissed water at the end of their garden, and swam refreshingly. Offers of black coffee, new bread, figs, grapes, in an arbour, greeted my emergence. Some of the carabinieri – I was presented to several new ones – went on duty, or to groom horses, or to do house-work, but the others gave me pleasant companionship in the garden, or

51

down at the landing-stage where I cleaned my bark for the day, till
nine o'clock when the lieutenant examined me. He stood on one
side of a bare table, on which were the contents of my puparin, and
I on the other. The marshal with the written interrogation of the
previous night stood by his superior, who was a perfect gentleman.
I corroborated my statements as to paternity, nationality, age, profession, and about fourteen months' residence in Venice. Was I
not in fact – seeing that I was blond – an Austrian, or a German?
'Nossiornò,' I spat indignantly: 'I'm a friend of Italy, not one of
her dear (and loathed) allies.' The lieutenant eyed me. Was I not
a priest? (This, of course, was due to my unfortunate bonze-like
visage and natural tonsure.) No: I said. I had tried to be one, but
the clericalist authorities said that I hadn't a Vocation. I happened
to be friendly with some royalists called Sforza Cesarini in Rome.
The lieutenant had a slight grin. Why did I gad about the lagoon
alone in a little boat? Did I do it for a penance? No, for my proper
health and diversion, I answered. Didn't I know that it was very
periculous? O by George yes: but one took one's risks in all decent
games – it was our custom: I told him. But (and here he was to
stagger me) why did I have charts with all the depths marked?
Merely to shew me where I might safely take headers without
embedding my nose in the mud. But where did I get these charts
which were of the Italian Hydrographic Department? Why, of
course I bought them quite openly at Ongania the bookseller's in
Piazza San Marco. (I should say 'Markusplatz', since the occu-
pation of Venice by Germans and Austrians.) Hum! And now let us
go over my generalities again – I was born at London of the late
Rolfe James and Pilcher Ellen Elizabeth, by profession a writer
and forty-nine complete years of age. I frankly admitted it all. A
carabiniere was moved to testify suddenly 'Excuses, Sior Tenente,
but I do not give him forty-nine years: for this morning at seven I
being present, even I, he jetted himself into the canal to swim,
saying that it was his custom, and he appeared to me to have one
leg white and of a whiteness, the rest of him being browned by
the sun, and (with permission) I could not possibly give him more
than twenty-five to not more than thirty years of age.' I giggled. The
lieutenant reproved me: 'Signore, we know quite well, we others,
how to pay respect to the dignified position of literature, and it was
not necessary for you to seek the respect due to old age as well.' To

which there was nothing to be said and I piously looked down my nose. But what was this about a white leg? Oh, I always wrapped a towel round my left leg, while sunning myself after bathing, just to have some proof handy that I really was a white man by nature. *Etsiansi omnes ego non*, has always been my rule of conduct. They seemed to think me a slightly eccentric person, but harmless so far. And now, was I known to anyone in Venice? Oh yes. The English Consul knew me: the English doctor knew me –. The lieutenant shook his head: yes, yes, but was I known to any Italians? I think he imagined the Consul and the doctor capable of supporting the spy on forts which I was suspected of being: so I said that I was an effective member of the Bucintoro Rowing Club. Ah, well, they could telephone there at once for information. And they telephoned. And, by the mercy of the gods, the person who answered them was the youth Fausto Levi, whom (as I said, by the mercy of the gods) I had been able to tip rather lavishly the day before. He confessed that they knew Sior Rolfé (they always accent my silent l and my silent e and call me Rolfé. which I think sounds beastly familiar,) quite well there, he being a most oh but most respectable sior revered for his mansuetude and very illustrious genius by everybody. And that finished it. The lieutenant settled himself into position and saluted me, announcing that I was free to depart without a stain upon my speckless character.

The friendly carabinieri gathered up my goods, attended me to the landing-stage, helped me to apparel the puparin, saluted my Union Jack when I hoisted it, effusively saluted me, and we parted the best of friends – a friendship which I found of the greatest possible service when, later on, I got into other difficult circumstances. And I rowed away straight for the Armenian island of San Lazzaro on the road back to Venice, mentally registering vows to throw away my photographic camera as soon as I got home, and never to go near their forts again, or to do anything whatever likely to offend the touchy darlings any more. But, do you wonder, O most affable reader, that I should love these dear Venetians?

Toto

'Yes, excellency.'

'And now, speak to no one, but send your mother to me, and tell her to bring ten or twelve respectable women who can sew. Say that I shall want them to stay in the palace for three or four days and that I will give them twenty lire apiece.'

'Yes, excellency.' And the lad went off with a graceful stride.

Toto was the gardener's son. He lived in a little cottage just outside the gates. He was nearly fifteen years old, a beautiful brown boy with long muscular limbs, hardy and strong, and the devoted slave of the House.

The Princess was an Englishwoman, proud as Lucifer of her own country, and devoted to Italy, in which she had lived since her marriage thirty years before.

It was a time of war and tumults. Italy had awakened out of a long sleep. Diplomats of other nations spoke contemptuously of her as 'a land of the dead', 'a mere geographical expression', but she had awakened now, and was about to draw adverse factions together, to unite them in one irrefragable bond, and to take an illustrious place among the great Powers of Europe.

Sant Angelo was a little white town, about twenty miles from Rome. It ran up the side of the hill and culminated in the palace of the Princes of Sant Angelo. The Garibaldians were encamped in the vineyards at the end of the gorge beneath, and though they dealt hardly with the townsfolk, no man had ever dared to molest the Princess. Her husband had died in the embrace of Our Lord, her two sons were fighting their country's battles in the North, and she was left alone with her women in the stately palace. The Garibaldians were supposed to be on the way to besiege Rome in the spring of the year, but the road was blocked by the Neapolitan army six miles off, as unwholesome a set of rascals as ever polluted this fair land. The Garibaldians were not all one could desire but the Neapolitans were worse, and Sant Angelo was therefore far from being a desirable place of residence.

It was winter time and an almost incessant *tra montana* shrivelled up the land with its icy blast. If you know what a Scotch North-East wind is and multiply it by ten, you will have some idea of the *tra montana*. Three days in each week it snowed, and then came the coldest of cold winds and froze the very marrow in one's bones. The Garibaldians were badly armed and their clothing was of the most meagre. No one liked them, but it must have been a heart of stone which could behold unmoved their patient sufferings, exposed to every wind that blew during that dreadful winter. Several died, – died of cold.

What little the townspeople could do, they did, – it was only a little. The frost and the frost-bitten soldiers were the only topic of conversation. By degrees, the news got into the palace and the ladies in waiting spoke of it when they sat around the great copper *scaldino* in the Princess's ante-chamber.

'The soldiers were dying of cold.'

'What,' said the great lady, her generous heart always full of pity for the sufferings of the poor, 'men dying of cold at my very gates?'

'Alas yes, excellency,' cackled the chorus.

The Princess stuck her needle into her tapestry and left the room. She muffled her head in a shawl and went, as quickly as her age would allow, to the palace gates. Toto had been to the greenhouse, and on seeing the Princess he ran to open the gate.

'Toto,' she said.

'At your service, excellency.'

She thought a minute looking into his face.

'You can be discreet and silent, Toto?'

'Yes, excellency.'

'I can trust you to serve me faithfully?'

'With my life, excellency,' said he and a glorious flush mantled his glowing skin and his brown eyes flashed under their straight delicate brows.

'You may get into danger.'

'For you, excellency,' said he with a look of adoration, and he kissed her hand.

'You will do exactly what I tell you?'

'Yes, excellency.'

55

'And now, speak to no one, but send your mother to me, and tell her to bring ten or twelve respectable women who can sew. Say that I shall want them to stay in the palace for three or four days, and I will give them twenty lire apiece.'

'Yes, excellency.' And the lad went off with a graceful stride.

Now the Princess, being an Englishwoman and the daughter of an English peer, was in the habit of doing good to the poor and needy. And she always kept by her several bales of English flannel.

In half an hour's time Toto presented himself bringing his mother and a posse of women. The Princess led the way to her stores. The bales of flannel were brought up into the picture-gallery, her excellency wielded a pair of scissors and cut out shirts and the women sewed them. Toto hung about, threaded needles and made himself generally useful. All the women in the palace were pressed into the service, meals were sent up into the gallery, and little else was done but the shirt-making. When night came there were nineteen shirts finished.

Then Toto was let out of a little door in the wall of the palace gardens away from the town and made his *gita* down the cliff by a zigzag path to the Garibaldian camp. He climbed and ran like an antelope.

'Warm shirts,' he gasped, for the way was steep and the burthen heavy, 'from the Princess – tomorrow I bring some more.'

And he darted away into the blackness of the night.

Next day more shirts were made, and taken to the camp by the indefatigable boy. The third day he ventured out by daylight and as fast as a bundle of shirts as large as he could carry was ready, he descended the cliff through the blinding snow with his burthen.

The next day he did the same, but when he came back late at night from his fifth journey he announced that there was a rumour in the camp that the Neapolitans were edging towards Sant Angelo.

The fifth day he left the palace at noon but immediately returned saying that the Neapolitans were in the gorge at the foot of the cliff and the shirts might perhaps be lost. 'But I can get there in the dark,' he said, 'and I will go all night.'

At 6 p.m. he made his first attempt. At 8 he returned. The Princess made him rest an hour and at 9 he started again.

At 11 the watchers in the palace heard a shot fired and half an hour after in walked Toto as cool as a cellared melon. 'Yes, they fired at me,' he said, 'but I lay flat on the ground and said fifteen Hail Maries.'

At 2 in the morning he went out for the last time.

He never returned.

The Princess herself sat up to watch for him. Four, five, six o'clock, but he came not. His mother sat and rocked herself to and fro. The Princess sat by her, held her hand and tried to comfort her.

The little town awoke with the yellow winter dawn.

The Princess offered a thousand lire for news of the lost boy.

The day passed and nothing was heard except that a detachment of Neapolitan cavalry had galloped towards Rome and that the rest of the squadron were gone back to the place of their previous encampment.

The coast being clear the Princess herself went in the evening down the cliff and along the gorge to the Garibaldians. She explained in a few words to the commandant, who she was and how the boy who had been her messenger was lost. Then she went back.

In a few minutes the story passed round the ranks and the men were told off to search for Toto.

Another night passed slowly and painfully to the distracted mother.

In the morning two Garibaldians desired an audience of the Princess. Toto was found.

I have said that the town of Sant Angelo was situate on the side of a hill with the palace at the top. On the farther side of the palace was a deep gorge with a precipitous cliff forming the opposite boundary. On the top of this cliff, within 100 metres of the palace was a little ruined tower. At daybreak a soldier had seen a cloth fluttering in the window. With three or four of his comrades he ascended and found the entrance barricaded by heavy stones. On moving these the tower lay open and there they found Toto, entirely naked, and frozen to death.

He had been caught by the Neapolitans, his bundle of shirts discovered, and they had stripped every stitch of clothing from his beautiful body and blocked him up in the ruined tower. The cliff was steep as a wall and there was no escape. At the little window he had stood and where he stood he died, one lithe soft arm against the wall and his dauntless brow leaned thereon. A scrap of the shirt they had torn from him hung from the square brown shoulders to the rounded thigh. He rested on one foot, the other slender limb was advanced in his usual graceful pose. They thought he was alive when they found him for his attitude was nature itself, his grave bright eyes were fixed with a soft yearning on his home, his sweet brave mouth firm-closed with a half smile, he was dead. Frozen to death, in the magnificent prime of his youth, he had given his life in charity.

They brought him in his naked beauty and laid him like a lily in his mother's arms.

An hour after, a file of dragoons waited upon the Princess of Sant Angelo with an order that she should leave the country in twenty-four hours.

She asked if she might know her crime.

'Your excellency has held treasonable communication with the enemy.'

'Treasonable communication!' she exclaimed. 'I have clothed the naked if that be treason!'

'Your excellency has supplied the enemy with clothes.'

'They were dying of cold.'

'But your excellency sent them *red shirts*.'

'*It is true,*' she replied, '*the flannel did happen to be red, but I had no other, and men were dying.*'

And so the Princess of Sant Angelo went into exile.

Excommunicated:
A Human Document

I write this in the fervent hope that I may wound one Jesuit. I desire that some of his candid friends shall read to him what I have written; and give him pain. 'Revenge is a morsel for the Gods.' The world may say that I show myself insane when I attribute to this priest the power which I attribute to him here. I care nothing for what the world may say. I only wish to set down the history of the atrocious tyranny which I endure, that I may make my tyrant wince, and share the sufferings which he has put upon me.

'Excommunication means nothing now. In olden times, when the world was drowned in damnable idolatry, it was serious enough: but, in this enlightened nineteenth century, its power has waned, and it can do no harm.' These words of wisdom were uttered by the long man in a corner of the smoking-room. It struck me that there might be many people to agree with him. His point of view was such a very comfortable one. There was so much common-sense about it. So I skipped upstairs to my studio and made haste to write down my own experience of excommunication. I never like to lose a chance of drawing a line between myself and the Philistines.

Since July 1895 I have lived in a petty town of 3018 inhabitants, 67 of whom are Roman Catholic voters. The town of which I write is in Great Britain. I will not give its name. It is a stronghold of Calvinistic Methodism, but other religions flourish, and the aristocracy attends the Established Church. We Roman Catholics are persons of no importance, well known to the police, and dominated by our rector, The Reverend Carlos Belestudiante, an animal of Spanish extraction born in England.

In May 1897, after five months' forebearance and private litigation, I found occasion to differ from my Jesuit pastor about a business matter; and I took legal means to lead him into the paths of righteousness. This was the crime for which I have been afflicted with a Boycott and an Excommunication. The history of the crime is published in another place.

When my attorney asked Fr Belestudiante to name a representative who would accept service of my writ, the tyrant rushed across the road to make a new attempt to terrorize me. I heard his howls, referred him to my legal adviser, and made as though to close the interview. But, at the door, he shook me by the shoulder, – he has a habit of knocking people down, – and put a solemn curse upon me, in the course of which he swore, *by the God and St Scioquio, that he would burn my works in order that he might wreck my chance of winning fame or credit, that he would ruin me, that he would make me suffer, prevent me from ever earning a living, and have me hounded out of the town.* He had invited me to commit apostasy before. I am a working man. I have no regular income. I live upon my wits, that is to say upon my brains and my right hand. Having the tools, I study art, and that is my deliberate preference. But, when I cannot purchase paints, I take the nearest pen, and write little tales like this one. I so do because I want to live.

At the moment when my Jesuit cursed me, pockets were bare, bare, bare. I suppose him to have known of this – he knows most things – because his next essay at bending me, took the shape of causing me to be ejected from my lodging. It was a Roman Catholic house, where I did not owe a sou. For five and forty hours, that is until reinforcements reached me, I was stranded without a crumb of food or a drop of drink, but I supported life with cigarettes. During the next four weeks Fr Belestudiante evaded the legal challenge which I flung at him, and he employed the time in saying things to my discredit on the Altar, in damaging my reputation in the town (using cunning catchwords, such as 'living on his wits', whereby the simple folk were vastly prejudiced). He caused the parents of my studio boys to take their sons away from me, and all the while he whined to my attorney that he feared to face, and fight, me before a British jury. In the end he implored me to accept a compromise.

Now, at the same time when my affairs were in this condition, there was another Roman Catholic – a Prussian – living near me, and he, in his own sphere, was a victim of tyranny of Fr Belestudiante. I knew him for a drunken sot, and he possessed a pretty Protestant wife whose portion was a most unhappy one. He owned a little local journal and he said that I could help him in his difficulties. When every other Roman Catholic shunned me as though I were a leper, in consequence of Fr Belestudiante's curse, this Prussian proposed that I should find him means, and in return he offered to sell my productions, in the shape of art and literature, at a higher price than ever I could get, also to give me a third share of the profits of his business, as well as board and lodging. He showed me proof that, a certain sum of money being granted, his business could be made a great success, and his wife, as his decoy, added her entreaties to his. I said that we were evidently brothers in misfortune, and, as such, should stick together. And I agreed to grant him his request as soon as I should have finished with my Jesuit.

Well, then, after a month of raving slander, Fr Belestudiante wanted me to compromise. In the interest of peace – surely a most desirable thing, and the proffered terms being those which one could accept with honor, I let him have his way. Documents were signed. I paid, to my Prussian, the sum which he had named (it was all my little savings), I went to live in the new house which he rented and began a new chapter of my life. Understand that we had neither luxury nor comfort. To a large extent we had packing cases for furniture. Necessaries, like beds and basins, were hired. Oh, we lived in humble poverty, I promise you. And now I asked my Jesuit pastor to remove his Curse. In a quite Pecksniffian letter, he refused, and in less than a week we found that he had put my Prussian and his Protestant wife under the same ban as that which weighed on me. We were to be hounded out of the town.

In accordance with Roman Catholic custom we asked our tyrant to perform the Rite of Benediction on our new house, and he would not notice our request, so condemning us to live on the territory of daemons. Here was a serious matter for, we argued with ourselves, if a small thing like a Rite be denied, most certainly a great thing like a Sacrament will also be denied, and for seven months we were forced to live without confession or communion. I call that Excommunication *latae sententiae*, i.e. deprivation of the Sacraments without pronouncement of a formal sentence. We were scrupulously careful about hearing Mass, being determined that nothing, except a shut door, should keep us from fulfilling our religious obligations. All the time, we laboured severely and lived unostentatiously, hoping that something which we did not know would bring our Jesuit pastor to a better mind. It seems as though this course, which contained more than a suspicion of contempt, must have goaded Fr Belestudiante to fury, for he began a series of manœuvres against our property and our lives. He was persuaded that his celluloid collar was a halo, and his Roman stock the Divine Aureola, and, on the strength of these, he claimed the privileges of his Creator to kill or make alive. There is no doubt of that. So soaked was he in slavering adulation that our simple silent scorn stung him to the heart. When we met him on the street our pastor turned his back. His curate did the same. It was the admiration of the town. Occasionally they came and stared in at our blindless windows, which abutted on the street, or they sent devout females to do so. We were made to feel like prisoners with a gaoler's eye upon them, and that indeed we were. Fr Belestudiante corrupted and intimidated our work people till they refused to serve us and so he brought our business to the brink of ruin. He sent artfully polite messengers to borrow our belongings. When I granted his requests he refused to give me back my own and so he robbed me of my tools of trade. He falsified accounts. Naturally enough his congregation copied him. His collectors and apparitor touted for subscriptions to our journal. They had no authorization but they kept the money. Before I was cursed many Roman Catholics had borrowed things from me and they declined to restore them now. My Roman Catholic landlady kept my winter clothes and made me shiver through the cold weather clad in summer lightness. My Roman Catholic short-hand writer kept my manuscripts and burned them. If the rector could do these things, they said, why should they not follow his example? A Protestant Urban Councillor let me amuse myself with his camera, and he took a severe scolding from our largest Roman Catholic, who alleged that any courtesy shown to me would be highly displeasing to Fr Belestudiante.

Why did we not prosecute these thieves? Listen, and I will tell you. We complained to the Bishop, and his Lordship said 'Keep out of the Courts, and do not raise a scandal.' So we obeyed, like meek fools, and exposed ourselves to further outrages.

Complete social ostracism was our lot. Life became a horror. Pen three people in one little house, render all their labour void, deny them the company of their species, and the distractions of religion, and what can you expect? My Prussian took refuge in beer, and neglected business. He never sold a single one of my productions. I was the salesman. His wife nagged and grizzled and grew ugly, and she cursed the Catholic Faith. For want of money which had gone in drink and drunken schemes, we suffered hunger. Food was very scarce. I have been a Roman Catholic for thirteen years and have learned to starve as well as any man, but my poor Prussian and his wizened wife grew thin and thinner. We lived on pittances of bread, potatoes and tea-leaves stewed, and stewed again, till they were fawn-color. When the diet was impossible we took a country walk, perhaps twice or thrice a week, and ravished blackberries, and nuts, and mushrooms from the woods and fields. For tobacco we tried to use an evil-smelling twist (ouf), and when that also failed we dried the fawn-colored tea-leaves and mixed them with wild thyme. Oh, how horrible it was.

All the town knew of our condition. Roman Catholics said, 'See what comes of disobeying the priest!' Protestants said, 'See what a dreadful thing it is to be a Roman Catholic!' And they all looked on with glee. We were like interesting strange wild beasts to them. They were amused to see us writhing in our chains. We made appeal in form to the Bishop of the Diocese, to the General of Jesuits, the Cardinal Prefect of Propaganda, and the Pope himself, and no one moved to stay our persecutor's hand. We were to be hounded out of the town, and what would have been the good of going away since we were to be prevented from earning a living, ever?

After four fearful months I revolted. It was September 1897. I said that my Prussian and his wife were being made to suffer on my account for Roman Catholics had written to tell me so. I said that I would go away and leave them free. I went away to another country for three months. I earned my living and, oftener than once a week, I sent moneys to my Prussian and his wife that they might live also, for I thought that it would be highly incorrect to desert them altogether. During those three months that brutal Jesuit maintained both Boycott and Excommunication with added rigour and severity for he had the direct co-operation of the Bishop now. Nothing would satiate him but that we should leave our business (which he coveted) for him to seize while we went, naked and homeless, to another town. He said so, and, finally, he killed our journal. He had been robbing us all along of advertisers and subscribers. Since June 1897 we had published with great difficulty, and, in October, we could not find a farthing for the printers. About this time we received another invitation to commit apostasy. My poor Prussian wallowed in his beer, spending some sober moments in futile Football Competitions. His wife haggard and shoeless went from one hysterical tantrum to another.

Seeing all my sacrifices to be of no avail I thought the end was near. I really did. Fr Belestudiante held a strong position. He enjoyed full meals four times a day. He had a crowd of backers, clerical and lay. He was adored – adored. He had but to launch an innuendo from the Altar for slaves to tumble over one another in their eagerness to win his favour. He paid them well. He was harassed by no necessity of working for his living. On the other side, for each mouthful of coarse food and drink I had to struggle with stiffened hands and tired brain – hard bitter thankless labour. I could not fight my foe on equal terms, for he held all the weapons. And, every morning, the Most Holy deigned to feed him on the Altar, while I was forced to kneel, aloof and shunned, at a distance near the door. I thought the end was near. The notion of surrender never crossed my mind. I was resolved to struggle till I died. But I considered that if death were really due it would be tidy to die upon the doorstep of my Jesuit pastor. With a man, a man can deal, sometimes a man may move a woman, but who can make a miscreant of the third sex feel? Yet I thought that even a Jesuit's spleen could not withstand the wants of one craving nothing but Viaticum. I suggested this to my Prussian and his wife and they agreed with me. Therefore I returned from my useless voluntary exile.

It was December 1897 when I came back to my prison, to potatoes and stewed tea-leaves. I shuddered in the cold wind and my summer clothes. As Christmas-time drew near, Excommunication became unbearable. To be denied the consolation of religion as well as the actual necessities of life, at such a season, was most terrible. We addressed a fresh appeal for justice to the Bishop, and to our Jesuit's immediate superior. We said that we had been refused our Rites for seven months and we asked how much longer the scandal of our persecution would continue. In reply the inexperienced Bishop did a shameful thing. He tried to baffle us, and to put us in a false position, by juggling with the words which we had used. He pretended to think that 'Rites' was a synonym for 'Sacraments', and he haughtily required of us the dates on which the Sacraments had been refused. We speedily assured him that his stratagem had been detected, and we added that we no longer needed his Lordship's services, giving what follows as our reason. Within three days from the posting of our appeal, the Jesuit Superior of Fr Belestudiante sent a priest to confer the Rite of Benediction on our house.

Here was a point gained. It had taken seven months to gain it and I won new courage from the victory. Now that the Rite had been conceded the road to the Sacraments lay open. I would explore it. If I reached my goal then I should be Excommunicate no longer, and then, perhaps, the Boycott and the Curse would be withdrawn. I could but try.

On Christmas Eve I went to confession to my Jesuit Persecutor. It was my way of intimating that I was setting malice on one side. He heard my tale of sin. Briefly, he gave me a petty penance and absolution. Then still throned upon the tribunal of penance and vested with the stole of jurisdiction he sardonically insisted that I must leave the town. He made that a condition upon which, alone, he would allow me to 'get on'. Those were his exact, but vulgar, words. I said simply that I looked upon the time and place as being most unsuitable for the present conversation. I wished to cultivate my soul, just then, and I left him in his confessional.

On Christmas morning, I heard three masses, making communion at the second – the first communion during eight months. It was not a sacrilegious communion in spite of that Jesuit's effort to slay my soul with Anger, but my heart was cold, apprehensive of ill, unresponsive, frozen in despair. Yet I had done my best.

At the beginning of the new year, 1898, I sent a note to Fr Belestudiante, saying that while I willed to yield perfect obedience to him in spiritual things, I would submit to no dictation regarding my secular affairs. And I refused to leave the town.

Another three months of hand-to-mouth existence passed, but how I do not know, and it was Eastertide. To die in mortal sin is to descend to Hell. Once more my will was good, and once more I made appeal to Fr Belestudiante, to the young Bishop and to his Jesuit Superiors, asking whether I should be allowed access to my duties, unmolested by a repetition of the unwarrantable dictation of the previous Christmas. There was no reply, and, to me, their attitude conveys that I am to be barred from the Sacraments, until I submit and go away. I believe firmly that right is on my side, but I admit the possibility of my being in the wrong, because my spiritual pastors will not guide me. Till they do I walk according to the light I have. And I should be a craven to sneak away and let a Protestant town see that a half-bred Spaniard and a Jesuit can, and does, wield the power to quail a British subject who will not pander to his whining. No, I will not submit to bullying, ecclesiastical, and quite immoral.

Early in the summer of 1898, a brighter light began to dawn upon my fortunes. I could not do as I should like to do and study art for the Jesuit stole my tools. But never have I been without a pen, nor have I allowed that pen to rest, and now at last, exiguous patient toil began to win reward. At midsummer fortune's face smiled even more entrancingly. Up to the moment I had given my private earnings to my Prussian and his wife. It was very little but it was all I had. And now the lady begged me not to give her husband any more because he would earn nothing for himself or for her as long as I provided him with money for his drunken bouts. Also, she prayed me not to quarrel with him. A woman can always turn me round her finger. I do feel so sorry for a woman. And I did as I was told. No more, no less. My Prussian chose to take umbrage, and his wife's wedding ring to pawn for beer. He demonstrated a talent for ingratitude and incorrect behaviour. He declared me to be a peacock and that he would bring me to my knees – bring me to my knees! He went outside to say so and I answered not a word. I offered money to his wife, but her husband would not let her take it. I was to ask him, as a favour, to accept my earnings! Finding that I opposed an adamantine front against his devious dirty efforts to bring me to my knees – to bring me to my knees – the stupid sot dismissed me from his house (oh, how glad I was to have my freedom given), abased himself upon the boots of Fr Belestudiante, became his abject slave and humble pensioner, was admitted to confession and communion, and thenceforth reeled about the town filled bung-full to the eyes with never-ending beer.

As for me, it gave me joy to think that I had stung that Prussian into doing something for his living, and for his most undeservedly unfortunate wife, and I was happy in being clear of a couple of silly disagreeable cadgers who got upon my nerves distracting me from serious work. But here, again, I was not acquainted with the powers wielded by my Jesuit pastor. Needing a new house I applied to several lodging-house keepers, Roman Catholic and Protestant. Thanks to my being Excommunicate the Roman Catholics refused me and the Protestants, in Fr Belestudiante's pay, did not reply to me. At last I found a resting place where I have lived since last July.

No sooner was my Jesuit aware that I was rising in the world, in spite of all his machinations of fourteen months, than he began to think, perchance, I might be pecuniarily worth consideration. Oh, I promise you, this Jesuit may be trusted to perform kowtow before a very tiny calf of gold. He actually wrote and asked me to make peace.

Now my temperament is far too indolent for a bloody man of war. Give me peace, and comfort, and warmth, a climate and pleasant smells and I am quite content. But when I had reviewed the damage which I had done to my Jesuit, and that which he had done to my mind, body and estate and reputation, in the ruthless, furious strife, which rages still since May 1897, when I remembered also the exceeding supple, subtile, sly, unscrupulousness of him and the improbability of his cherishing an honest desire for an equitable arrangement, with no back-thought of scoring a diplomatic triumph, or driving a one-sided bargain – when I remembered all this, I considered that some definite arrangement, something of the nature of a protocol, should be drawn up and signed, and I asked him to formulate his conditions or terms. Observe the grace with which I conceded that right to his reverence.

After dilly-dallying till the end of August 1898, he refused to do as I suggested. He would delude me with false peace, and tie my hands, but that I told him of my utter disbelief in the *bona-fides* of his application, and returned forthwith to the *status ante quo*.

Since then fresh priestly efforts to dislodge me have been made. With no success. I feel like the prisoner tied to the gunpowder barrel. I don't know when the inevitable catastrophe will come. I loathe the place. Even Protestants know me now for a person who may be plundered with impunity. The saturnine Fr Belestudiante and his Roman Catholics are their great exemplars. The town photographer dare not take my photographs. The Deputy Coroner and Chairman of the School-Board have not scrupled to borrow a set of valuable books in yellow bindings and refuse, in writing, to return them. The otherwise respectable bookseller begs of me a dozen copies of my lately published book for sale, accepts my terms, declines to pay in cash or kind, and will not restore my dozen books. These marauders know that by their vile tricks they help my Jesuit pastor to carry out his threat – that he will prevent me from ever earning a living. How can I earn a living with brigands always buzzing about me when I want to work? They help to make my life so intolerable in their snivelling little town that I shall run away in pure disgust. Not Queen Victoria but a half-bred Spaniard and a Jesuit rules here, and even Protestants are not too proud to be the jackals of a Jesuit, if by cringing they may curry favour with him. They know me to have neither time nor means, nor inclination, to prosecute them, and they are not ashamed to take advantage of my generous courtesy, or to plunder the results of my unceasing toil. Naturally it is my warmest wish to quit the town, where I am used so scurvily, where the hand of every man opposes me, and where my hand is against every man's. It is the most bestially disagreeable place I ever saw.

Fr Belestudiante has made three and a half years of my life entirely miserable. Two years while I was in his employ, buoyed by promises which he dishonoured, and a year and a half boycotted, excommunicated, and a common lucky-bag. He has robbed me of the fruits of my labour of those years. I call that the equivalent of a thousand pounds. He has created for me a fictitious and undesirable reputation, robbed me of my health, deprived me of human sympathy, barred me from the Sacraments, defiled me with a nameless stigma, and he has sworn to prevent me from ever earning a living. No matter how strenuously I work (and the whole town knows me to be indefatigable), no matter how squalid and ascetic a life I lead (and the whole town knows that too, by reason of my living in a public place with ever-open doors and windows), this Jesuit's Boycott and Excommunication will deprive me of the amenities and considerations which I earn. Why should I persevere in a useless struggle? I should do better for myself to be a thief, a drunkard or a lecher, and take pay, as the favoured free Roman Catholics here are and do. But I disdain dishonour.

Now hear me.

I gibbet Fr Belestudiante of the Company of Jesus, and defy him.

If he can drive me to the workhouse, I go with joy. To prison, I go with joy. To the grave, I go with joy and without fear.

But, by the aid of the gods who are my patrons, and of my angel-guardian, I shall not die, but live to see the repentance of Fr Belestudiante. And when, by this pen which that foolish Jesuit forces me, against my will, to ply, I shall have earned two thousand pounds, when the Boycott together with the Excommunication and all Canonical Censures shall have been removed publicly from me, when I shall have been readmitted, by my Jesuit, to the Sacraments – then I shall consider that my reputation has been cleared, and that I have proved all Fr Belestudiante's menaces to have been merely the way in which a frantic theologian expresses himself, and nothing more. I shall have resisted the devil, and he will have fled before me.

I will rest content . . . all the bitter agony of . . . of mind which I endure because of him. Then, not only will I leave the . . . town, but the country also. And I will retire to my castle of . . . in Aria, to bury myself in my beloved study and for ever after hold my peace. God send that soon!

But, until then, here I am; and here I stay.

In Praise of Billy B.

This is nearly the true story of the Row at Magdalen.

There was a Magdalen man who decided to pose as an aesthete. He was a nasty little skunk with depraved tastes, disgusting habits and a vitriolic tongue. The naked legs and muscular *torsi* of the boating men filled him with envious longing for what could never be his. Like the fox who said he didn't want the grapes, he never spoke without some cut or gibe at those whose healthy physique and wholesome virility should have made him blush for his own puny insignificance.

His sarcasms when Magdalen got to the head of the river, passed all bounds of decency; and at the bump-supper the boating men, who were certainly a little intoxicated with their athletic successes and other things, resolved for once to take the law into their own hands and make the little beast rue his insulting words. The idea was a charming one, and a rush was made for the New Buildings where the miscreant had his lair. His rooms were lighted, but there was no response to the invitation for him to come out and meet the athletes he had vilified. A search was made, but the aesthete was nowhere to be found.

Now you must clearly understand that had the DISGRACE TO HIS SEX been forthcoming the athletes would probably have had their halfpenny worth out of him: either by cutting his long, greasy, and perfumed hair, or by dangling him at the end of a string from the little bridge in the Water Walk close at hand, or by making him run round and round the quad attired in a sage-green billycock, a pair of Oriental slippers, a peacock's feather, and nothing else, the night being warm for the time of the year.

The idea was simply to give the animal an unhappy quarter of an hour.

Disappointed in this laudable desire, there was only one course open to the athletes. They proceeded to make hay of his furniture.

A haycock was formed of the chairs and tables and heavier furniture in the middle of the room, and the interstices were stuffed with books and pictures. A china pot crowned the summit wreathed with a garland of sham sunflowers. Sheets, counterpanes, curtains and rugs draped the ceiling-reaching pile, and at its base there was a cycle of pots and pans filled with water and with a choir-boy's photograph floating on each surface.

Around this haycock the athletics danced hand in hand with artless glee, singing boating songs.

In the midst of it all the aesthete came home. Hearing the noise as he went up the stair, he began to suspect something. On arriving at his own half-open door he took a cautious peep before declaring his presence.

What he saw frightened him so dreadfully that he ran away.

All the rooms on his own stair were dark, and there seemed no refuge for the fugitive. Mad with fear he tore along the portico and up a neighbouring staircase. Seeing a light under a door he dashed into the room of he knew not whom and with gasping sobs besought the occupant to save his life.

Now the man whose premises were thus unceremoniously invaded was neither an athlete nor an aesthete. He was a reading man who took pains with his personal appearance and was faultless in his attire. Athletic exercise he enjoyed in reason, and he was an accomplished musician. He was a well-bred good-natured man of the world, and later on he distinguished himself by taking a Triple First and a college fellowship. He made the palpitating aesthete comfortable in an easy chair, gave him some benedictine and cigarettes and set to work to console him and make him a cup of tea.

The aesthete said he was his saviour, described in lurid lights the danger he was in, and wept with terror and gratitude all over the fireplace. The said saviour whom we will call Billy B. tried to cheer him up, and was giving him good advice for his soul's health, when lo and behold, the athletes who, having finished their haymaking, had perceived the light in Billy B.'s room, came thither to relate the deed which had been done. The aesthete grew livid again, and begged permission to retire behind the curtains which hung before the window. He disappeared, and the next instant Billy B. was calmly entertaining the athletes. He fed them with curious drinks and tobacco in various forms, and as each hero confessed his share

71

in the haymaking the aesthete behind the curtain took down his name and words.

It was perhaps a couple of hours before this pleasant party broke up, and the conversation had drifted into other channels to such an extent, that when the last athlete took his departure Billy B. had completely forgotten the presence of the aesthete behind the window curtains.

He went into the bedroom to wash his hands, and then sat down for half an hour of Balzac before going to bed, but as he drew his chair nearer the lamp his memory came back again, and he went and looked for his aesthete. That person was nowhere to be seen, and Billy B. very naturally concluded that he had found an opportunity of slipping off while his foes had their attention otherwise engaged.

The next morning there were shocks.

The Warden sent for certain athletes, and charged them with having committed an outrage on the previous evening in the rooms of Mr Simone Memmi Simpkinson. He was appallingly definite in his details. 'You, Mr A., did this, and you, Mr B., did that,' and so on through the whole bag of tricks. Nothing was ever more complete.

The athletes were given the option of denying the charges, or of defending themselves; and of course there were no denials.

Some mention was made of a 'lark', not by way of defence but of explanation.

'Sending down' was the natural sequence. No one was a bit surprised at that, but everybody did want to know who had sneaked to the Warden. The general feeling was in sympathy with the athletes, and it was argued that the only people who had the power to give such definite information to the Warden as had undoubtedly been given, were Billy B., the aesthete, and the athletes themselves. It was ridiculous to suppose that the athletes would give themsleves away; the aesthete had not been seen by anybody during the function in his rooms; there remained only Billy B., and, as soon as an opinion had had time to be formulated, he fell under a good deal more than suspicion of being a filthy little sneak who had accepted the confidences of the athletes and then betrayed them to the Warden.

This suspicion soon betrayed itself in a very unpleasant way for poor Billy. Men gave him the cold shoulder, and in a very little while he began to realize that he had received the Order of the Cut. The reason of it never entered his head; and as he was a proud sort of beggar he made no attempt to enquire.

When the aesthete saw that Billy was cut, he cut him too. This did gall Billy and he asked him what the devil he meant by it. The aesthete meekly explained that he was only carrying out the advice Billy himself had given on the night of the haymaking, and he was endeavouring to copy the manners and customs of the majority in the college. He said further that he was much obliged to Billy for letting him stay behind his curtain and collect the evidence which he had given to the Warden, that he had remained in his hiding place until the last athlete had left and then slipped away during Billy B.'s temporary absence in the bedroom, and he asked for Billy's congratulations on the completeness of the revenge which he had been able to take.

Billy B. was horrified. He said several things; and he asked the aesthete if he intended to allow the college to cut him (Billy) for his own dirty tricks. The aesthete faltered out that he thought Billy wouldn't mind, that it wouldn't last long, and then he cried, and begged Billy not to ruin him.

Billy B. took him by the nose and shook him till he shrieked. Then he said that as the college had done him the injustice of suspecting him of sneaking, and had cut him without asking if he could defend himself, he should not deign to ask for a hearing now. If Simpkinson was so lost to all honourable feeling as to allow a perfectly innocent man to suffer for his misdeeds, he (Billy) disdained to suggest to such a vermin what his duty was.

And there the matter stood. Billy B. accepted the situation with a haughtiness which caused a good deal of surprise, and wrapped himself up in his books. As I said, he has since taken a Triple First. And he did not wear his heart upon his sleeve for daws to peck at.

He endured this martyrdom for a year. At the end of that time the aesthete left the place, and the real facts became known. Whether Billy B.'s heroism had been noticed by the Warden and he had, in common justice, compelled the aesthete to own up in writing (as he did), is not exactly known, but anyhow there was no one more affected and surprised than Billy B. at the dénouement and at the revulsion of feeling which took place in his favour.

73

The Bull Against the
Enemy of the Anglican Race

We, in the Name of God, Hadrian the Seventh, the Paparch, the Apostle of the Apostolic See and of the Roman City, by Divine Clemency reigning, wish to make known to all to whomsoever these presents shall come that a certain Anglican, by name Nicholas Crabbe, a student of human and divine affairs, a lover of his Motherland, excellent in reverence toward his King and toward the Roman Office of Blessed Peter Prince of Apostles, has exposed to Us the iniquity of an individual by name Domnus Aluredus de Ulmeto de Sancto Petro, a baron of the United Kingdom and proprietor and editor of a journal called *Katheemerangereion*, denouncing the said baron as an hysteriamonger and enemy of the Anglican Race in that he (swayed by a proper devil) insidiously disseminates exciting things, on six mornings of each week in the United Kingdom and Anglia Overseas, and on seven mornings of each week among Anglicans and others on the Continent of Europe, secretly sapping the virility and triturating the solidity and upsetting the gravity of the race of Anglicans. For, as is well-known, the said Anglican Race has been distinguished for pre-eminence in the sterling qualities of virility and solidity and gravity during the last four centuries at least. But, now, this denounced baron, presumptuous cultivator of hysteria, diabolically engages in weakening and emasculating and harassing and embarrassing and distracting and impeding the moral fibre and the intellectual operation and the physical fortitude and the psychical equipoise of individual Anglicans old and young and male and female, in Anglia and in all Anglican dominions on this orb of earth beside elsewhere.

Wherefore, the said Nicholas Crabbe, desirous of restringing the unutterable iniquity of the said Domnus Aluredus de Ulmeto de Sancto Petro before the time when the said admirable Anglican character shall have been by him ruined irretrievably, has deprecated Us that We should most grievously molest the said baronial hysteriamonger by damning him with the javelins of Our apostolic maledictions

Whose petition benevolently receiving, We, Hadrian the Paparch, a plebeian lifted from the stercorary and placed above princes, being as prompt and eager to reward and dignify all plebeians and patricians possessing aristocratic affections as We are swift and fierce to abuse and abase all patricians and plebeians possessing ochlocratic affections, have done the said maledictions in manner following, with other matters thereto pertinent, all written by the proper hand of Lord Ermenegildo, Our archbishop and cardinal-deacon of Saint Vitus the Dancer and his Companions Martyrs.

And We have done the said maledictions cordially because Our Sacred Congregation of Timeetephimeridoon, having studied certain piles of the said journal *Katheemerangareion* with the denunciation of the same written by Our well-beloved and trusty son Nicholas Crabbe, has reported to Us these particulars:

i. The denounced journal is on sale everywhere (continent of Europe and overseas included) for the insignificant sum of one halfpenny, whereby a very vast sum (indeed in pride it is alleged the largest) circulation is secured:

ii. Concerning the content of the said journal, the Fathers of Our said Sacred Congregation have judged it to be comparable with the content of a sink or a gutter or a sewer, where everything which is atrocious and shameful and ridiculous and vain and inane and useless and exasperating and inflammatory and noxious and so forth collects and is celebrated, infecting the vicinity. An example by way of a favour – for the said baronial proprietor and editor, pursuing his diabolical machinations against Anglican Virtue (namely, against the Sum of the Psychical and Intellectual and Physical Excellences of Anglicans,) yelled about Massacres in Pekin when no massacres were there, and, moreover, he (forsooth) temerariously attempted to teach the grandmother of Anglican universities (widow of polite letters) to suck eggs, sending a naive credulous representative to be hideously inebriated and commodiously deluded (on matters connected with Ragging) by earnest ingenuous members of Our college of Saint Mary Magdalene:

75

iii. And the said Fathers of Our said Sacred Congregation have laid at Our feet a categorical analysis of the content of the said journal of the last ten years, wherein is demonstrated nothing conducive to the soul's salvation or the body's sanity or the true culture and equipoise of the mind, but solely histories of horrors, catalogues of crimes, administrations to vanity, promulgations of agitating notions, fulsome flatteries of certain smart persons (generally meretricious and particularly vulgar,) extremely unintelligent anticipations under the name of news with their subsequent shameless refutations, deliberate lies done diurnally for dirty dross.

Since the three-times and four-times accursed invention of the art of printing, and its application by the turpilucricupidous (baronial or otherwise) primarily to the gain of gold and secondarily to the gain of power, both by means of the concupiscence of human nature ever (as Saint Paul says) avid of some novelty, it has been the custom of Our apostolic predecessors (from Alexander the Sixth, the Paparch, of magnificent invincible memory) to muzzle these devils of printers by censures, maledictions, excommunications, interdicts, and all commodious anathemas. Whose example We are not slow to follow; and We will make a mild beginning, while reserving far more awful fulminations for the reduction of incorrigibility.

It is not essential, either to temporal politeness or to spiritual progress, that Christians should know or note the gests of mummers, buffoons, misers, innkeepers, gladiators, snobs, bounders, the criminal classes, or the set fatuously dubbed smart, all self-damned. Still less is it desirable that Our well-beloved children should upset their own equanimity by the perusal of gasped and snipped and hiccoughed canards, or torpidify their divinely-donated faculties by reading feuilletons of great dramatic power, vilely and cheaply printed. None of these things, nor indeed aught of like kind, ought to concern Christian men and women by one jot or tittle. For such matters are of the earth, very earthy in fact, inevitably tending to dull dirtiness. And ye, well-beloved wearers of white robes, ye are but *metoikoi*, resident aliens on this orb of earth for a very little while, and having nothing whatever to do with it, excepting to keep yourselves unspotted from its filthy contaminations.

Perpend, then, it is Our will that ye perpend well, these, Our hard sayings, that your free intellects may willingly assent to and sanction and gladly confirm Our commandments.

Far be it from Us to deny (for We are not yet quite blind nor entirely stupid nor more tedious than Our apostolature involves) that there are journals which do purvey news of the kind which is fit for printing, conveniently ordered, and embellished with such expositions of salient events (in the shape of leading articles) as may assist the formation of correct opinions. Such journals are produced by persons of liberal learning and good manners and special knowledge, who merit (and receive) Our approbation for that they are diligent (according to their lights) in honourable business and do not abuse their powerful position for the sake of personal advantage, but are content to toil late and early and arduously and very nobly at paltry pittances never exceeding three-thousand pounds sterling a year. And such journals are, *Times, Weekly Edition of Times, Morning Post, Pall Mall Gazette, Globe, Punch, Saturday Review, New York Times, Boston Transcript, Populo Romano, Gazzettino di Venezia, Sior Tonin de Bona Grazia,* and *Figaro de Paris.* And it is Our will, well-beloved children, that ye shall select these and these only, as commodious for your safety, when concupiscence of reading journals shall molest you.

Moreover, by way of giving a concrete expression to Our apostolic detestation of the infamy of the said Domnus Aluredus de Ulmeto de Sancto Petro, a baron of the United Kingdom and proprietor and editor of the said journal called *Katheemerangareion,* We will erect a rampart for defence from and for offence against his infernal onslaught.

Wherefore, We, by these presents, do create and constitute and confirm a new Order of Chivalry, under the Candid Protection of Saint Gabriel Archangel and News-bringer, and having the following Fundamental Constitutions:

i. The Candid Order of Saint Gabriel Archangel and News-bringer shall consist of a Grandmaster, and a Company of Knights and Ladies, and a Company of Esquires and Women:

ii. The Grandmaster of the said Candid Order is the Roman Pontiff, in whom is vested the absolute sovereignty and sole government of the said Order:

iii. The Grandmaster may select six knights and six ladies of sympathy and discretion for His counsel and comfort, and such knights and ladies are to be called Knights-Magnates and Ladies-Magnates respectively having precedence in the Order next after the Grandmaster:

iiii. Knights and Ladies of the Candid Order of Saint Gabriel are all such baptized Christians who shall have sworn the Greater Oath of the said Order confirming the same with their names and sigils, and who shall have been inscribed in the Golden Book of the said Order with a record of accolade:

v. Esquires and Women of the Candid Order of Saint Gabriel are all such baptized Christians who shall have sworn the Lesser Oath of the said Order confirming the same with their names and sigils, and who shall have been inscribed in the Silver Book of the said Order:

vi. Here followeth the Greater Oath of the Candid Order of Saint Gabriel: I (name) now swear, to Almighty God and to Saint Mary the Virgin and to Saint Peter Prince of Apostles and to Saint Gabriel Archangel and News-bringer and to You Lord (name) Grandmaster of this Candid Order, promising obedience, that I will never knowingly read or touch or see or hear the journal called *Katheemerangareion*, owned and edited by Domnus Aluredus de Ulmeto de Sancto Petro, and that I will never knowingly permit it to be brought into or remain in any place from which I can reject it, and that I will never knowingly remain a moment of time in any place where it may be: So help me God and Saint Mary the Virgin and Saint Peter Prince of Apostles and Saint Gabriel Archangel and News-bringer:

vii. Here follows the Lesser Oath of the Candid Order of Saint Gabriel: I (name) now swear to Almighty God and to Saint Mary the Virgin and to Saint Peter Prince of Apostles and to Saint Gabriel Archangel and News-bringer and to You Lord (name) Grandmaster of this Candid Order, promising obedience, that I will never knowingly permit the journal called *Katheemerangareion*, owned and edited by Domnus Aluredus de Ulmeto de Sancto Petro, to be brought into or to remain in any place from which I can reject it, and that when (swayed by the devil) I am constrained to read the said journal I will read it in a secret place with shame dispersing it immediately after such reading in an efficacious and suitable manner: So help me God and Saint Mary the Virgin and Saint Peter

Prince of Apostles and Saint Gabriel Archangel and News-bringer:

viii. The Cross of the Candid Order of Saint Gabriel is a Cross Ansata in burnished silver having its outer angles intagliate with four flaming lilies: the Cross of Esquires and Women shall have a length and breadth of two centimetres: the Cross of Knights and Ladies shall have a length and breadth of four centimetres: the Cross of Knights-Magnates and Ladies-Magnates shall have a length and breadth of six centimetres: the Cross of the Grandmaster shall have a length and breadth of eight centimetres: and all Crosses may be worn on a gold riband of tissue four centimetres in width or on a gold chain one centimetre in width:

viiii. The Vexillum of the Candid Order of Saint Gabriel is an oblong of two squares of gold tissue, one square insigned with the Cross of the Order within a bordure of flaming lilies, the other cut into six streamers powdered with flaming lilies, cross and bordure and powderings being of silver tissue:

x. Our well-beloved and trusty son Nicholas Crabbe and all Our bishops and all Our heads of religious communities throughout the world are required to swear and to transmit to Us as Grandmaster the Greater Oath of the Candid Order duly signed and sealed within ninety days and ninety nights from the date of this present constitution: failure will produce a summons to the Apostolic Threshold to hear a word:

xi. Our well-beloved and trusty son Nicholas Crabbe and all Our bishops and all Our heads of religious communities throughout the world, having qualified as aforesaid for inscription in the Golden Book of the Order, are to be taken as duly accoladed, and are named Knights-Founders and Ladies-Founders respectively of the said Order, and they will instantly enrol and accolade Knights and Ladies and enrol Esquires and Women in accordance with these present constitutions:

xii. And We name Our trusty and well-beloved son Nicholas Crabbe Our Locumtenens and Signifer of the Candid Order to hold and to exercise the said offices without let or hindrance as long as he shall behave himself well.

The foregoing are the Twelve Immutable Fundamental Constitutions of the Candid Order of Saint Gabriel Archangel and News-bringer, ordained and promulgated by Us Hadrian the

Seventh, the Paparch, the Apostle of the Apostolic See and of the Roman City, the Founder and First Grandmaster of the said Candid Order, by Divine Clemency reigning.

Finally, a spirit of pastoral love even for an errant and obstreperous ram, and a certain sense of neatness and decency, constrain Us to clear away rubbish from the bulwark herein erected against diabolical invasions, and to afflict preliminarily with a few dire things the said Domnus Aluredus de Ulmeto de Sancto Petro, baron of the United Kingdom, proprietor and editor of the journal called *Katheemerangareion*, arch-hysteriamonger and Enemy of the Anglican Race, as follows:

By the Authority of Almighty God, and by the potency of Blessed Peter Our Senior to whom was given the power of binding and loosing, and by Our Own ministry also, let the said Domnus Aluredus de Ulmeto de Sancto Petro be excommunicate and anathema and alienate from the thresholds of the Holy Church of God, unless he comes converted to satisfaction. And let the maledictions written in the Old and New Testaments come upon him, unless he comes converted to emendation. And let him be accursed in his editorial and printing and publishing offices, and in his barony, and in counties, cities, castles, fields, forests, roads, and let the earth be unviable by him, and let the sea and all waters be unnavigable by him, and let the air be unvolitable by him, and let him be deleted from the book of the living, and let him not be inscribed among the just, unless he repents and comes to satisfaction and emendation. Let it all be done. So We ordain: so We command: let Our will be a sufficient reason.

Given at Rome at Saint Peter's on the Vatican Hill, and sealed with the Ring of the Fisherman, this sixty-ninth day of Our Supreme Pontificature.

L.S. (*Signed*)   Hadrian P.M. vii

(*Countersigned*) ✠ Mario Card. Secr. L.S.

              ✠ George Card. Vicecanc. L.S.

              ✠ Robert Card. Poenit. L.S.

              ✠ Ermenegildo Card. Dat. L.S.

Notes on the Conclave

The Death of the Pope

When Leo Pontifex Maximus XIII, Ruler of the World, Father of Princes and Kings, Earthly Vicar of Jesus Christ, shall have reached the end of his life in this world, he will receive absolution and a plenary indulgence in the article of death from Cardinal-Penitentiary Antonio Agliardi.

Before the College of Cardinals assembled at his bedside, he will make his final profession of faith. While he is in his agony, by ancient custom the pontifical nephews and familiars participate in his effects.

The Verification of Death

When he has submitted to the laws of mortality, the Cardinal-Chamberlain Luigi Oreglia di San Stefano, in a violet cappa, attended by the clerks of the apostolic chamber in black, thrice will tap the cadaver on the brow with a silver mallet, invoking the dead Pope first by his pontifical name *Leo*, secondly by his christian name *Gioacchino Vincenzo Rafaele Luigi*, thirdly by the pet name by which his mother called him in babyhood, *Nino*. When no sign of life ensues, apostolic prothonotaries, kneeling, write the act of death, and record the vacancy in the Paparchy.

Pontifical Sigils and Inter-Pontiff

The Fisherman's Ring, called 'The Little Peter in a Boat', of massive gold worth 100 crowns, is taken from the dead hand by Cardinal-Chamberlain, broken, and divided among the caerimonarii. All other sigils are delivered by the Apostolic-Datary to the Cardinal-Chamberlain, and destroyed by him in the presence of the Auditor and the Treasurer. The Cardinal-Chamberlain (as Cardinal-Dean of Bishops), assisted by Cardinal-

Prior-Presbyter Netto (the Patriarch of Lisbon), and Cardinal-Archdeacon Luigi Macchi, assume the government of the Church.

Evisceration

Within twenty-four hours the cadaver is eviscerated by Drs Lapponi and Mazzoni. The viscera, extracted through a slit in the carotid, are enclosed in a sealed crystal vase; and deposited in the Church of Sts Vincent and Anastasius by the Fountain of Trevi, in accordance with the Bull of Leo XII, AD 1824.

The Lying-in-State

The cadaver is embalmed, washed, shaved, and pontifically vested by the Penitentiaries of St Peter's, who place a mitre on the head and a chalice in the hands. It is deposited on a lofty bier in the Trinity Chapel of the Vatican Basilica, with the feet protruded through the grille for the osculations of the faithful.

Sepulture

On the third day, the cadaver is put into a lead coffin with a medal from each cardinal of Leo XIII's creation; the shell is included in a cypress coffin, and immured by torchlight over the second pillar in the left aisle of St Peter's, next to the tomb of the Stewarts. Here it must remain for at least one year before its translation to the permanent tomb already chosen. The expenses are borne by the Apostolic Chamber.

The Novendialia

On the first and ninth days after the death of the Pope two hundred requiems are intoned, the first and last by a cardinal-bishop assisted by four mitred cardinals; on each of the other seven days one hundred requiems are intoned.

The Conclave

On the tenth day, cardinals from all parts of the world reach

Rome: the mass of the Holy Spirit is intoned, a sermon is preached by some eloquent friar, and, surrounded by the Swiss Guard, their Eminences go (singing *Veni Creator Spiritus*) to the cells which they are to occupy till they have elected a Pope. Cardinal Oreglia's cell is hung with green, because he is a creature of Pius IX. All the other cells are hung with violet, because their inhabitants are creatures of Leo XIII. Each cardinal's armorials are blazoned over the entrance to his cell. A bed, a table, and a chair are all the furniture.

The Immuration

After taking possession of their cells, their Eminences adjourn to the Pauline Chapel to hear the reading of the pontifical Bulls directing elections. Until three hours after sunset, ambassadors of sovereigns, and the people, have access to the Conclave. Then the heralds shout 'All out'; the doors are shut, all doors and windows are bricked up, and all chimneys (except one) are capped. The outer door is locked on the inside by the Cardinal-Chamberlain, on the outside by Prince Chigi, the Hereditary Marshal of the Holy Roman Church. Sick conclavists may retire this way, but they may not return. Apostolic prothonotaries record this immuration as an Act of the Conclave.

The Conclavists

Every cardinal is attended by a chaplain and a valet. Cardinal-princes, such as Kopp of Breslau, and infirm cardinals, such as Capecelatro of Naples, may use two body-servants. There are also a sacristan with sub-sacristans, masters of ceremonies, secretaries with their servants, a Jesuit confessor, a physician, a surgeon, a pharmacist, a mason, a carpenter, with their respective boys, and a host of domestic prelates and menials. All these take a stringent oath of secrecy.

Food and Drink

passes into the Conclave by a little turn-table near the principal door. It is all rigorously examined by Cardinal-censors to detect letters or communications surreptitiously sent to their Eminences

83

by externs. The rigour of conclavial seclusion has been relaxed on very important occasions. In the Conclave of 1800, on the Isle of St George by Venice, an Englishman, named Oakley, was permitted to enter, for the purpose of delivering to the Cardinal Duke of York the announcement of King George III's intention to provide that 'august personage' with an income of £4000 per annum.

The Sistine Chapel

Here are erected thrones for the cardinals: green for Oreglia, violet for the rest. The canopy of each throne is demissible by a cord. Silver basins full of voting papers stand on a table before the altar. On the altar is a huge gold chalice covered by a paten.

Modes of Election

The new Pope is elected *By Compromise* – that is, when the cardinals nominate certain of their number as Compromissaries with power to name the Pope; or *By Inspiration* – *i.e.*, when two-thirds plus one of the cardinals present shout the name of a certain cardinal, 'Svampa is Pope', or 'Gotti is Pope'; or *By Adoration* – *i.e.*, when the minimum majority of two-thirds plus one spontaneously proceed to adore a certain cardinal (Leo XIII was elected in this way); or *By Scrutiny* – *i.e.*, when each cardinal secretly records a written vote; or *By Accession* – *i.e.*, when, the Scrutiny having failed to give the minimum majority to any cardinal, the opponents of the cardinal whose tally is the highest shall accede to him.

Eligible Persons

In theory, the election of a Pope is a patent manifestation of the operation of the Holy Spirit; and *Ubi Spiritus ibi Libertas*. Hence, not only all cardinals, but also all baptized males are eligible for the Paparchy. The first Pope, St Peter, was not a cardinal before his nomination. John XII (955–963) was a youth of eighteen. Benedict IX (1033–1048) was a little boy of ten (*puer fere decennis*).

The Form of the Voting Paper

Of the *Scrutiny* (inside):

```
Ego Cardinalis
.  .  .  .  .  .  .  .  .  .  .

Seal                        Seal

Eligo in Summum Pontificem Reverendissimum
Dominum meum Dominum Cardinalem
.  .  .  .  .  .  .  .  .  .

Seal                        Seal

.  .  .  .  .  .  .  .  .  .
.  .  .  .  .  .  .  .  .  .
```

Of the *Accession* (inside) the same words as above, except that the middle compartment contains the words: '*Accedo Reverendissimo Domino meo, Domino Cardinali.*'

Of the *Scrutiny* and *Accession* (outside):

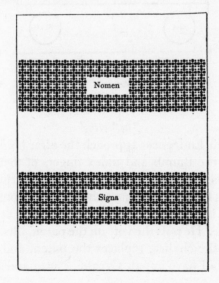

These voting papers are about a hand's breadth in length, and half as broad. The cardinals, seated each on his throne, disguise their writing, and take the most meticulous precautions against being overlooked. At the top, each elector writes his own name, folds it down and seals it at the two appointed places. In the middle he writes the name of the baptized male (cardinal or otherwise) whom he is moved to elect; and this portion he does not fold over. At the bottom, he writes his own motto; folds it up, and seals it at the two appointed places. Nothing now is visible save the name of the person to whom the vote is given, and the back of the paper is heavily engraved so that the name of the voter and his motto shall not be read through it. Such a voting paper when filled up might appear as follows:

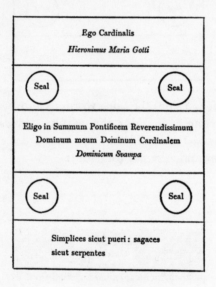

Ego Cardinalis
Hieronimus Maria Gotti

Seal   Seal

Eligo in Summum Pontificem Reverendissimum
Dominum meum Dominum Cardinalem
Dominicum Svampa

Seal   Seal

Simplices sicut pueri : sagaces
sicut serpentes

The Voting

One by one their Eminences approach the altar holding aloft their votes between the thumb and index fingers of their ringed right hands; aloud they severally swear: 'Before Christ the Lord, who is to be my Judge, I attest that I have chosen him whom I judge fittest to be chosen, if it be according to God's Will; and at the Accession I will do the like.' He puts the vote on the paten, tilts the last till the vote slips into the chalice, replaces the paten, and reverts to his throne. When all have voted, Oreglia, Netto and Macchi bring the chalice down to the table, from which the silver basins have been removed. A ciborium, empty, is placed beside the full chalice.

The Scrutiny

The names of all the cardinals are written on little snips of parchment. Each snip is rolled up and placed in a hole in a lead ball. The balls are put into a huge violet burse. The junior Cardinal-Deacon (Felix Cavagnis?) shakes it, draws out three, and the names written on these three snips are the names of the Cardinal-Scrutators, who now have charge of the voting. They watch the full chalice, while the Augustinian sacristan at the altar intones the mass of The Holy Ghost. Then, the said chalice is vigorously shaken by the Senior Scrutator. The Junior Scrutator counts the votes from the chalice into the ciborium; and, if the number of them does not correspond with the number of cardinals present, they are burned, and the voting is repeated. All being correct, the three Scrutators sit at the table in face of the College; the Senior Scrutator takes the votes one by one, reads his name to whom the vote is given, passes it to the next Scrutator, who silently reads and passes it to the Junior Scrutator, who proclaims the name, and files the vote on a needle threaded with a skein of violet silk, piercing the word 'Eligo'. Each cardinal records each suffrage on a printed tally.

The Accession

If no cardinal has obtained the minimum majority of two-thirds plus one of the number of electors, recourse is had to Accession (of which the form has been given), in order that their Eminences may have a chance of amending their suffrages by acceding to the cardinal whose tally in the Scrutiny is the highest. The Accession papers are filled, deposited, ceremonially shaken, solemnly surveyed, proclaimed, filed, and recorded on tallies, as in the Scrutiny.

The Post-Scrutiny

The Senior Cardinal-Scrutator takes the Accession papers of him whose tally is highest. Of these, he opens the lower part, silently comprehends the seals and mottoes, passes each one to the next Scrutator, who does likewise, and passes the document to the Junior Scrutator, who proclaims both seals and mottoes and records them on a list. The same is done with the votes of the Scrutiny; and, if it be found that any cardinal has voted for one and the same in both Scrutiny and Accession, then the latter is nulled. The top of the votes only is opened by the Senior Scrutator, under observation of his coadjutors, in order to settle discrepancies. These functions are performed twice daily, after morning mass and after evening hymn to The Holy Spirit, until such time as that the Church is provided with a valid and legitimate Paparch. Each time that a Scrutiny or an Accession is declared futile, the votes are burned on a bundle of straw in a stove whose chimney extends into the Piazza di San Pietro, where the Romans are used to watch for the puff of smoke; and, on seeing it, they go home, saying 'Domeniddio sends us no Pope today'.

Factions and Veto

Formerly, the Holy Roman Emperor, the Catholic King of Spain, and the Christian King of France claimed the right of vetoing the election of cardinals who appeared likely to be disagreeable. At present there is no Roman Emperor, for the last (Francis II) resigned that style on assuming the title of 'Austrian Emperor' in August 1806. The German Emperor, William of Hohenzollern, pious magniloquent grandson of the Divine Victoria, might become 'Caesar Semper Augustus' (if he were Catholic) on the death of the present Austrian Emperor. Meanwhile, the Catholic King of Spain is a foreign hobbledehoy and quite impotent; and there is no Christian King de facto of France. Wherefore it may be said that European politics will not influence the Conclave of 1904. The conflict will be between the will-power and ambitions of individuals, or between ecclesiastical factions. In the latter event, its object will be the destruction of United Italy, and the reconstruction of that Temporal Demesne of the Paparch which the magnificent invincible Alexander VI won at the sword's point, which his successor, the diabolic plebeian Julius II, with the sword's keen edge consolidated, and which Pius IX lost by the fortune of war to Victor Emanuel II of Savoy in 1870. The Church appears determined publicly to compete with the world. The arts of holy living and holy dying may be practised privately. The factions in the ensuing Conclave will be but two in number – Spiritual and Temporal – and 'Christ guides the barque of Peter so that she never can sink', said the exquisite St Antonine of Florence (whose quality all the world admires and loves) at the election of Calixtus III four hundred and fifty years ago.

The Elect Apostle

When at last, by Inspiration, Adoration, Scrutiny, Accession or Compromise, a Pope is elected, the act of the Conclave is recorded by apostolic prothonotaries; and all the cardinals sign and seal it. Cardinal-Archdeacon Macchi and the second Cardinal-Deacon Steinhuber the Jesuit demand the Elect's assent to his own election. His Holiness is conducted to the rear of the altar, where he indues himself with pontifical habits (three sizes are provided to suit the stature of any Pope): a cassock of white taffetas with cincture, a fair white linen rochet, the pontifical stole, a white skull-cap, an almuce of crimson velvet and ermine, shoes of crimson velvet embroidered with gold crosses, and a new Ring of the Fisherman for his index finger. He is placed in a chair before the altar; and the Cardinal-Dean of Bishops demands of him the new name by which he will be known. [The custom of taking a new name on assuming the Paparchy arose with Sergius III (904–911), whose proper name was Pigface (Osporci).] Each cardinal releases the cord of his canopy, which falls down; for, in the presence of Christ's Vicar not even an Emperor may remain covered. The conclavists proceed to pillage the cell lately occupied by His Holiness.

Adoration

This function should not be misconstrued by those whose pre-dilection is to think ungenerously of the Ancient Faith. The Adoration is rendered to God, whose Vicegerent here on earth is the Pope, the Vicar of Christ, the successor of St Peter and of Cæsar; to which last divine honours were paid. Cardinal-Arch-deacon Macchi lifts the Supreme Pontiff on to the altar of the Sistine Chapel; and, in their order, the cardinals kiss the cross on his shoe and the ring on his hand, and receive the kiss of peace over both shoulders. If, by chance, at the moment of his election the Pope should lack Holy Orders, he is ordained deacon and priess and consecrated bishop by the Cardinal-Dean. For the Pope it Bishop of Rome.

Proclamation

The mason breaks open the walled-up door; and the Cardinal-Archdeacon there proclaims, 'I announce to you great joy: we have for a Pope the Lord Cardinal (Domenico Svampa) who wills to be called (Pyrophenges the First).' In the ages of faith this proclamation was repeated on the balcony of St Peter's, and there the Pontiff imparted Apostolic Benediction to the City and the world. At his election in 1878, Leo XIII wished to observe this order: but his curial prelates, anxious not to bless the Golden City where reigned the Sabaudo King Humbert the Martyr, informed the Pope that the window of the balcony (closed since 1870) could not be unfastened; and practically hullabalooed and hustled His Holiness into St Peter's.

Incoronation

The insignia of the apostolate are the Fisherman's Ring, the Keys of Heaven and Hell, the Triple Cross, the Triple Crown, Tiara, or Triregno. The Pope receives the Ring at his election. A few days later, he is crowned by the Cardinal-Archdeacon in the basilica of St Peter's-by-the-Vatican. On the morning of his incoronation he is awakened by a procession of curial prelates who gravely ostend the bronze figure of a crowing cock in remembrance of the fall of his first predecessor, St Peter. In the Sistine Chapel he is vested for mass in red, with precious mitre of gold and gems. Preceded by seven acolyths with seven candles and the triple cross, he descends to St Peter's. At the Holy Door he receives the homage of the Chapter. At the Gregorian Chapel he receives cardinalatial and prelatial homage. Ambassadors and hereditary princes join his train. The Hereditary Princes-Assistant at the Pontifical Throne, Colonna and Orsini, walk at his right and left, equally placed lest, in view of their immemorial, interminable, incomprehensible, hereditary feud, they should fight for precedence.

The Four Lavations

The Pontiff washes his hands four times. At the first lavation, water is presented by the Conservator of the Roman People; at the second, by the Generalissimo of the Pontifical Army; at the third, by the Ambassador of the Christian King of France; at the fourth, by the Ambassador of the Roman Emperor. Who is now the Conservator of the Roman People? King Vittoremanuele III de Savoja? Who is now the Christian King of France? Don Carlos de Bourbon, or Prince Louis Napoleon Buonaparte, or Monsieur Emile Loubet? Who is now Imperator Cæsar Semper Augustus? The pious, magnanimous William of Hohenzollern? The Father of princes and kings alone can say.

Sic Transit

The paraphernalia of God's Vicegerent glitters with gold and gems. All that this earth holds of best and mightiest ministers at his footstool. And this is the moment when the meanest acolyth of the court holds up before his eyes a bunch of flax, lights it, and, as it flames and dies, intones: 'Behold Most Holy Father how the glory of this world passeth away.'

The Mass of Incoronation

Seven huge candles are lighted on the pontifical altar, beneath the giant baldaquin of gilded bronze, three on each side of the crucifix, one behind it. The Pope says the *Confiteor*, ascends the throne, and the Cardinal-Archdeacon invests him with the pallium (which he at all times will wear in sign of universal jurisdiction), saying: 'Receive the Sacred Pall, the plenitude of pontifical office, in honour of the Lord God Omnipotent, of His most glorious Virgin Mother, of the blessed Apostles Peter and Paul, and of the Holy Roman Church.' After the *Gloria*, the Cardinal-Archdeacon, with a crowd of Consistorial Advocates and Auditors of the Ruota, descends beneath the altar by the ninety-five ever-burning lamps to the shrine of St Peter, where he intones the versicle, 'Give ear, O Christ'. The weird inhuman voices of eunuchs of the pontifical quire respond: 'To our Lord the Supreme Pontiff, to the Pope by God decreed.' Again they supplicate: 'O Saviour of the world, hear him.' A Latin sub-deacon intones the Litanies of the Saints. On the altar, a Latin sub-deacon intones the *Epistle* in Latin; a Greek sub-deacon intones it in Greek. A cardinal-deacon intones the *Gospel* in Latin; another cardinal-deacon intones it in Greek.

Venom

After a Conclave there generally are some disappointed cardinals. When the Pope is to offer bread and wine, a sacristan brings three breads on a paten. The Pope selects one, lays it on the corporal of the altar, and watches the sacristan eat the two breads which remain. A crystal ewer of wine, and another of water, are presented. The Pope puts a little of both into the chalice, and watches the sacristan drink the remainder. After consecration, His Holiness elevates the Host to the four quarters of the globe, amid the clang of presented arms and the thrill of silver trumpets in the dome. When the Pope is to take communion, he ascends his throne, and cardinal-deacons bring the Sacred Host and the Chalice. Thrice he breaks the Host; one Particle he himself consumes, the cardinal-deacons eat the other two. An equal ceremonial is kept with the Chalice, in order that the Supreme Pontiff may not be envenomed in the Eucharist.

Honorarium

When the mass is ended, the Cardinal Archpresbyter of St Peter's offers to the Pope a white damask purse containing twenty-five gold crowns as 'honorarium for a mass well sung'. He deigns it to the cardinal-deacons who sang the *Gospel* in Latin and Greek; who, in turn, demit it to the *camilli* in lace and vermilion who bear the burden of their Eminences' trains.

The Triple Crown

Borne on his lofty throne, surrounded by flabellifers beating the incense-laden air with fans of peacocks' tails, the Pope goes to the balcony of benediction. Here the Cardinal-Archdeacon crowns him with the three-fold crown, intoning the tremendous formula, 'Receive this tiara, adorned with three crowns, and know thyself to be Ruler of the World, the Father of princes and kings, and on earth Vicar of Jesus Christ our Saviour'. Arising crowned, the Paparch imparts Apostolic Benediction: 'May Almighty God, Father, Son, and Holy Ghost, bless you'; and he retires into the Vatican, while two cardinals publish a plenary indulgence in Latin and Italian.

The Lateran Throne

As Bishop of Rome, the Pope's Holiness, either in person or by proxy, must take formal possession of, and be inthroned at, the cathedral of the Apostolic diocese. That cathedral is not the basilica of St Peter-by-the-Vatican, as vulgarly is imagined, but St John's *in Laterano, Omnium Urbis et Orbis Ecclesiarum Mater et Caput,* the most important church in Christendom. But this involves a resplendent progress through the streets of Rome, and no Pope has set his foot outside the Vatican since 1870 (except when Leo XIII was driven to the Barbarini palace and across the Via Della Zecca in 1890): nor will His Holiness emerge from this seclusion, so some say, as long as Italy remains United. Alas, then, the ensuing pageants will be deprived of much of their prefulgent splendour, and the obsequies of Leo XIII, with the election and incoronation of this successor, will be celebrated in obscurity and with mutilated rites.

Daniel on the Coming of the Messiah: Fragment of a Discourse

For one unaccustomed to write the Latin language with fluency, and possessing only a limited acquaintance with a subject of such importance and magnitude as the Prophecy of Daniel concerning the coming of the Messiah, it will be difficult to avoid, on the one hand, discussing the matter with inaccuracy, and on the other, trespassing on the writings of many illustrious men who have already treated so fully on the same subject. In the hope that I may fall neither into this Scylla nor into this Charybdis, and fortified with your reverence's command to write, I have written these words.

The archangel Gabriel being sent to Daniel when he was praying and mourning over the sins of the Jewish nation, spoke as follows:

'Seventy weeks are shortened upon the people and upon their holy city that transgressions may be finished and sin may have an end and iniquity be abolished and everlasting justice may be brought, and vision and prophecy may be fulfilled and the Saint of Saints may be anointed. Know thou therefore and take heed that from the going forth of the word to build up Jerusalem again, unto Christ the Prince, there shall be seven weeks and sixty-two weeks, and the streets shall be built again and the walls in straitness of time. And after sixty-two weeks Christ shall be slain and the people that shall deny him shall not be his. And a people with their leader that shall come to destroy the city and the sanctuary and the end thereof shall be waste and after the end of the war the appointed desolation. And he shall confirm the covenant with many in one week and in the half of the week the victim and the sacrifice shall fail and there shall be in the temple the abomination of desolation and the desolation shall continue even to the consummation and the end.'

This prophecy was delivered in the last year of the Babylonian captivity when Darius was reigning in the year 536 BC. Theologians teach that this prophecy applies to the coming of the Lord Jesus Christ, to His Sacrifice on Calvary, to the conquest of Jerusalem by the Romans under Titus, and to these alone. It remains then only, for the verification of this doctrine, to compare the terms of the prophecy with historical facts, and to do this it is necessary to consider it under four heads:

i. Of the interpretation of the words '70 weeks';

ii. Whether the title 'Sanctus Sanctorum' relates to the Lord Jesus Christ alone or to another;

iii. Whether what is prophesied of this 'Sanctus Sanctorum' relates to the Lord Jesus Christ alone or to another;

The rest is lacking

Suggestion for a Criterion of the Credibility of Certain Historians

The object of this essay is to impeach the veracity of certain writers hereinafter definitely named, except in so far as they are corroborated by indubitable authority, (e.g., original private letters, original records of sworn testimony, original acts of legal tribunals, etc., all contemporary,) or by the inherent probability of their statements; as well as of all writers unnamed, whose qualifications place them in the same category; and also, from the particular examples cited, to deduce a standard of universal application. The writers directly impeached are Stefano Infessura, and John Addington Symonds. A single point, common to both, viz., the accusation which they have laid against Xystus P.M. IIII, is selected as the ground on which their trustworthiness may be impugned.

This charge is so unspeakably deadly: for the merest whisper of it suffices to destroy; and its effect does not depend upon evidence of its truth. Most great men in the world's history have been its victims. At one or another time, they (inadvertently perhaps) have trodden upon some human worm; and the worm has turned and stung them. At one or another time, they have made an enemy, have scorned a woman, have offended the vanity of a minor man, have flouted a priest, (all three sexes equally are guilty); and, in revenge, the charge is made against their peace. It is the weapon with which Spite is wont to stab the back of Scorn. It invariably is directed by inferiors against superiors, by mediocrity against genius. It was as common nineteen hundred years ago, when C. Valerius Catullus denounced L. Aurelius Cotta the praetor, and M. Valerius Martialis derided the so-called Naevolus and Phoebus, as it was four hundred years ago, when Stefano Infessura defamed the Roman Pontiff, as it was in the Victorian Era, when John Addington Symonds defiled the memory of the dead. It often was and is found in connection with the clergy; sometimes urged by them against incommodious laics, sometimes directed by one clerk against another. It was and is used with the same frequency and hilarious inconsequence, (and merits as much attention), as the rabid screeching of antisemitic and anglophobic journals of the Gallican gutter. Generally, the good sense of human nature stamps out the foul thing in the moment of its inception. On occasion, it is permitted to survive; but it rusts unnoted – until some fiend refurbishes its sting, and slays. And, now and then, it at once is efficacious; and an innocent irretrievably is damned. There was a horrid example in Rome only seven and fifty years ago.

Gaetanino Moroni was a barber's son, born xvii October, 1802, who used to shave the Abbate Mauro Cappellari. The latter, noting him as a witty and teachable lad who was very anxious to improve his mind (*molto ingegno, moltissima docilità ed una smania vivissima d'istruirsi*), gave him opportunities of learning Latin and of associating with scholarly men. In 1822, at the age of twenty, he married Signorina Clementina Verdesi, by whom he had several children. In 1826, his patron was named Cardinal-Presbyter of the Title of San Callisto, and in 1831 succeeded to the pontifical throne by the name of Gregory P.M. xvi. Signor Moroni continued to serve him as personal attendant (*primo ajutante di camera*); and, in his leisure time during twenty years from 1820 to 1840, with the assistance of his master, as abbate, cardinal, and supreme pontiff, who placed at his disposal the Secret Archives of the Vatican and numerous other private collections of documents, he compiled the celebrated *Dizionario di Erudizione Storico Ecclesiastica* in 120 volumes in 8°, of which six are occupied by the index. This huge achievement, the fruit of unusual intelligence and industry, was begun when he was but a youth of the age of eighteen years, and done at a time when he actually was in the pontifical service. It should be unnecessary to point out that such mental and manual labour as this is incompatible with degenerate tastes or vicious habits. In 1846, Gregory died; and Pius P.M. ix, Who succeeded Him, listened to the voice of accusation, deigned credence; and dismissed Gaetanino Moroni at the age of forty-four years from the Apostolic Family. (Let is be noted that Gregory had not invested His familiar with the sacred purple of the cardinalature. That, in the eyes of Stefano Infessura and John Addington Symonds, would have been proof-positive of guilt.) Signor Moroni accepted ruin and disgrace with admirable serene disdain. He retired into private life; and studied fourteen hours a day during six and thirty years, living alone with his family on the second stair of Palazzo Carpegna in Via Degli Staderari, consoled sometimes by the society of two or three not unfaithful friends, until his death, iii November, 1883. His immense Dictionary remains the standard work of its kind. What other monumental works might the world have owed to this gigantic intellect – blighted in its bloom by calumny's venefic breath!*

Such, as has been said, is the paralysing nature of this censure that it brings condemnation even when unsupported by proof. The spleen of the accuser, of the Adversary, is gratified even when, or rather only when, conviction does not follow: for conviction is definite and final, and deprives of the pleasing spectacle of ruin done. Indeed, when the accuser is so fatuous as to be particular in his accusation, to make a detailed and circumstantial charge, then failure utter and complete sooner or later will become his portion, as in the present case of Stefano Infessura and John Addington Symonds.

Xystus P.M. iiii is the victim of these two historians. His Sanctitude was the victim of many defamers: for it was the habit of the time 'to treat the Pope as negroes treat their fetishes. If they had cause to dislike him, they beat and heaped insults upon him – like the Florentines who described' this very pontiff 'as leno matris suae, adulterorum minister, diaboli vicarius. On the other hand they really thought that he could open heaven and shut the gates of hell.'† On Ascension Day 1484, in illustration of the foregoing, Xystus was prevented by sickness from imparting Apostolic Benison at the Lateran Basilica; and the disappointed Romans scrupled not to curse Him Who was to have blessed them. A

---

* The material of this sketch was given verbally in 1890 to the present writer by the great and noble Duchess Caroline Sforza-Cesarini, *nata* Shirley, (natural daughter of Robert Sewallis Shirley, Viscount Tamworth, educated and bred by her grandfather, Robert, seventh Earl Ferrers, FSA, who made her his heiress, married, xvii September, 1837, to Duke Lorenzo Sforza-Cesarini, *cf. Annual Register*, 1837, p. 147) and by her eldest son, Duke Francesco Sforza-Cesarini, himself no undistinguished student of history, father of the present Duke Lorenzo II Sforza-Cesarini. Both Duke Francesco (O.I.B.Q.) and his illustrious mother (O.I.B.Q.) spoke from personal knowledge of the facts, of the two Popes, and of the victim of this dreadful accusation. *Cf.* also Silvagni, D., *La Corte e la Società Romana nei secoli xviii. e xix.* Firenze, 1882. 8°. 3 tom.

† Symonds's *Renaissance in Italy*.

particular accusation was brought against His Sanctitude in tangible and answerable, and in intangible and unanswerable form. The abominable epigram, said by Bernardino Corio in his *Storia di Milano* to have been placed on the tomb of Xystus, is a specimen of the latter, a specimen of the calumnies used by the faithful against the faithful in all ages, utterly rabid, utterly irresponsible, utterly intangible and irrefutable, and utterly sufficient to defile. The epigrammatist conceived a dislike for the Supreme Pontiff; and incontinent expressed his bile, compiling a catalogue, in verses that would scan, of all the most disgraceful sins known to casuistry, and ascribing them to his enemy in the usual manner. Cicero's distinction, 'Aliud est maledicere aliud accusare,'* was not and is not observed by writers of this kidney. It suffices for them to assert of an aged clergyman, whom all the while they recognise to be God's Vicegerent, as follows:

> *Fur, scortum, leno, moechus, pedica, cynaedus*
> *et scurra, et fidicen, cedat ab Italia:*
> *namque illa Ausonj pestis sceleratus senatûs*
> *Petrus, ad infernas est modo raptus aquas.*

But on the other hand, the accusation, as stated by Stefano Infessura, and iterated with additional suggestion by John Addington Symonds, is an exquisite example of a detailed and circumstantial charge, and therefore of a tangible and answerable charge, which historians of the eminence of Dr Creighton and Professor Pastor have considered, and denounced as baseless. It here is specially intreated of, with a view to the exhibition of Infessura and Symonds as being unworthy of belief (except when they are corroborated by probability or by proved authority): for it is maintained that the man or woman, who would make use of such a weapon for the gratification of spite or grudge or indeed for any cause whatever, should be held to be devoid of moral principle, unrestrained by conscientious scruple, and capable of any iniquity.

Stefano Infessura,† calling himself The Scribe of the Senate and

---

* Pro M. Coelio III.

† Truth often is revealed by unconscious indirections; and his motive, perhaps, may be detected in the italicised words of the following passage, which occurs on p. 158 of his scurrile journal. Nothing exasperates a mediocre journalist so much as indifference on the part of those whose acts are material for journalism, and Infessura's method of satiating chagrin is by no means unique:

'*Hic*' (i.e., Xystus) '*literatorum* et bonos mores habentium' (the pharisaical concate-

Roman People, records the accusation against Xystus in his *Diarium Rerum Romarum* (Ed. Tommasini, Roma, 1890), pp. 155–6, in the following terms:

...et quinta hora noctis mortuus est Xystus.... Hic, ut fertur vulgo, et experientia demonstravit, puerorum amator et sodomita fuit; nam quid fecerit pro pueris qui serviebant ei in cubiculo experientia docet; quibus non solum multorum millium ducatorum redditus donavit, verum cardinalatum et magnos episcopatus largiri ausus est. nam, cum non propter aliud, ut dicunt quidam, dilexisse comitem Hieronimum, et fratrem Petrum, eius germanum ac post cardinalem Sti Xysti, nisi propter sodomiam? quid dicam de filio tonsoris? qui puer nondum duodecim annorum continuo cum eo erat, et tot et tantis divitiis, bonis fructibus, et, ut dicitur, magno episcopatu decoravit; quem, ut fertur, volebat ipsum cardinalatum, contra omne genus iustitiae, etiam in pueritiâ promovere; sed Deus destruxit desiderium suum.

The terms, in which John Addington Symonds states the accusation, are that Xystus

could not enjoy life without some youthful protégé about his person. So, in 1463, he made his valet, a lad of no education and of base birth, Cardinal and Bishop of Parma at the age of twenty. His merit was the beauty of a young Olympian. With this divine gift he luckily combined a harmless though stupid character.*

Let the evidence be noted, upon which Stefano Infessura violated the Divine Commandment, *Thou shalt not revile the gods, nor curse the ruler of thy people.*† He based his calumnies on such pretexts as 'ut fertur vulgo', 'ut dicunt quidam', 'ut dicitur', 'ut fertur'. It is true that he adjoined to these 'experientia demonstravit', 'experientia docet': but he has not given notes of the experiment, nor has he furnished the names and testimonies of credible witnesses. His accusation confessedly is based upon the gossip and tittle-

nation is notable) '*inimicus*, solum illi grati erant mali. quare condita fuerunt, nescitur tamen per quem multa carmina in eum, quae sunt ista, videlicet:

'Leno vorax pathicus meretrix delator adulter
si Romam veniet, illico Croesus erit.
Paedico insignis, praedo furiosus, adulter
exitiumque Urbis, pernitiesque Dei.
Gaude, prisce Nero, superat te crimine Xystus;
hic scelus omne simul clauditur et vitium.'

* *Renaissance in Italy*, i. 327.
† Exodus xxii. 23.

tattle of an admirably scandal-loving court; and on this account alone it might be argued that a writer, who shamelessly conceived of his duty as historian to be the collection and the tabulation of kinaidic *on dits*, is unworthy of general acceptation; and the argument should gain importance from the fact that these loathsome calumnies, which so foolishly have been set down as serious history and, as such, embellished with definite terms, can be refuted with perfect and convincing facility.

Xystus P.M. IIII is arraigned as παιδεράστης and καταπύγων (the terms are too gross to be detached in the Roman character from their context). These are neither synonymous nor essentially inclusive; and Stefano Infessura, who would appear to have held the opinion that an aged sovereign cannot love his sisters' children, or advance his nephews' interests, nisi propter an unutterable reason, very clearly manifested an intention to proceed on the second term rather than on the first: for he has designated

(*a*) The pueros qui serviebant Ei in cubiculo, whom He rewarded with many thousand ducats, bishoprics, and cardinalatures;

(*b*) The comitem Hieronimum, et fratrem Petrum, eius germanum,* ac post cardinalem Sti̅ Xysti;

(*c*) The filium tonsoris, puerum nondum duodecim annorum, whom He decorated with an important bishopric, and wished to raise etiam in pueritiâ to the cardinalature contra omne genus iustitiae.

Here we have a concise accusation, the accuracy of which is susceptible at least of trial. Xystus reigned from 1471 to 1484; and it would be difficult, though not impossible, to obtain a list of clerks whom, during those thirteen years, He preconised to bishoprics: but His *Atti Concistoriali*, regarding the cardinals whom He pronounced, easily are accessible to the ingenious student. An inspection of this category, noting the ages of the porporati at date of creation (where it is possible to give them) will throw a strange light upon that unknown son of the barber and those unnamed pages of the bed-chamber whom Stefano Infessura included in the episcopate and Sacred College.

---

* I do not know whether this is eius germanum, i.e., own brother to Girolamo, or Eius germanum, i.e., His Own child. There was another calumny, emanating from clerks of Ferrara, to the effect that the mother of Xystus bore this Pietro to her son.

I. AT THE CONSISTORY OF 1471, Xystus P.M. IIII renounced two cardinals, who were:

1. Giuliano della Rovere, Cardinal-Presbyter of the Title of San Pietro AD VINCULA; (*he was the first Pontifical Nephew, a diabolic plebeian who subsequently became Pope under the name of Julius P.M. II, AD 1503*).

2. Pietro Riario, Cardinal-Presbyter of the Title of San Sisto; (*æt. 25; he was the second Pontifical Nephew*).

II. AT THE CONSISTORY OF 1473, Xystus P.M. IIII renounced eight cardinals, who were:

3. Philippe de Levis, Cardinal-Presbyter of the Title of Santi Marcello e Pietro; (*æt. 38*).

4. Stefano Nardini of Forli, Cardinal-Presbyter of the Title of Sant' Adriano; (*he had been thirteen years Archbishop of Milan*).

5. Auxias de Podio (Despuig), Cardinal-Presbyter of the Title of San Vitale; (*æt. 50*).

6. Pedro Gonsalvo de Mendoza, Cardinal-Presbyter of the Title of Santa Maria IN DOMNICA; (*æt. 45*).

7. Giambattista Cibo, Cardinal-Presbyter of the Title of Santa Balbina; (*he became Pope under the name of Innocent P.M. VIII, AD 1484*).

8. Antoine Venier, Cardinal-Presbyter of the Title of Santi Vito e Modesto; (*æt. 51*).

9. Giovanni Arcimboldi, Cardinal-Presbyter of the Title of Santi Nereo ed Achilleo; (*he had been preconised Bishop of Nocera in 1468*).

10. Filibert Hugonet, Cardinal-Presbyter of the Title of Santa Lucia IN SILICE; (*he was a Burgundian*).

III. AT THE CONSISTORY OF 1476, Xystus P.M. IIII ascribed five to the College of Cardinals, who were:

11. Jorge da Costa, Cardinal-Presbyter of the Title of Santi Marcello e Pietro;* (*he already was Archbishop of Lisbon*).

12. Charles de Bourbon aîné, Cardinal-Presbyter of the Title of San Martino AI MONTI; (*he already was Archbishop of Lyons*).

---

* Iteration and reiteration of these Titular Presbyteries is due either to the death or promotion of the previous occupant. As well as the three ranks of Deacon-, Presbyter-, and Bishop-Cardinal, the various Titles themselves are of higher or lower grade; and promotion or exchange will cause a vacancy.

13. Pietro Ferrici, Cardinal-Presbyter of the Title of San Sisto; (*æt.* 61).

14. Giambattista Millini, Cardinal-Presbyter of the Title of Santi Nereo ed Achilleo; (*æt.* 71).

15. Pierre de Foix cadet, Cardinal-Presbyter of the Title of Santi Cosma e Damiano; (*æt.* 27).

IIII. AT THE CONSISTORY OF 1477, Xystus P.M. IIII renounced seven cardinals, who were:

16. Cristoforo della Rovere, Cardinal-Presbyter of the Title of San Vitale; (*æt.* 42; *he was the third Pontifical Nephew*).

17. Girolamo Basso della Rovere, Cardinal-Presbyter of the Title of Santa Balbina; (*he was the fourth Pontifical Nephew*).

18. Georgius Hester (or Kesler), Cardinal-Presbyter of the Title of Santa Lucia IN SILICE; (*he already was Bishop of Brixen*).

19. Fra Gabriele Rangoni of the Religion of the Friars Minor, Cardinal-Presbyter of the Title of Santi Sergio e Bacco; (*he was Ablegate to Imp. Caes. Frid. IIII Semper Aug. and to King Matthias Corvinus of Hungary*).

20. Pietro Foscari, Cardinal-Presbyter of the Title of San Niccolo INTER IMAGINES; (*he already was Bishop of Padua*).

21. Don Juan de Aragona, Cardinal-*Δ* of Sant' Adriano; (*æt.* 14).

22. Rafaele Galeotto Sansoni-Riario, Cardinal-*Δ* of San Giorgio IN VELUM AUREUM; (*æt.* 16; *he was the Pontifical Grand-Nephew*).

V. AT THE CONSISTORY OF 1478, Xystus P.M. IIII nominated one cardinal, who was:

23. Domenico della Rovere, Cardinal-Presbyter of the Title of San Vitale; (*he was the fifth Pontifical Nephew, and already Abbot of Vercelli*).

VI. AT THE CONSISTORY OF 1480, Xystus P.M. IIII renounced five cardinals, who were:

24. Paolo Fregoso, Cardinal-Presbyter of the Title of Santa Anastasia; (*he already was Archbishop and Duke of Genoa*).

25. Cosmo de' Migliorati Orsini, Cardinal-Presbyter of the Title of Santi Nereo ed Achilleo; (*he already was Archbishop of Trani*).

26. Frédéric de Cluny, Cardinal-Presbyter of the Title of San Vitale; (*he already was Bishop of Tournai*).

27. Giambattista Savelli, Cardinal-Δ of Santi Vito e Modesto; (*æt.* 62).

28. Giovanni Colonna, Cardinal-Δ of Santa Maria IN AQUIRO; (*æt.* 23).

VII. AT THE CONSISTORY OF 1483, Xystus P.M. IIII renounced five cardinals, who were:

29. Giovanni de' Conti, Cardinal-Presbyter of the Title of Santi Nereo ed Achilleo; (*æt.* 70).

30. Frère Eloy de Bourdeille of the Religion of the Friars Minor, Cardinal-Presbyter of the Title of Santa Lucia IN SILICE; (*æt.* 77).

31. Juan Moles de Margaritis, Cardinal-Presbyter of the Title of San Vitale; (*æt.* 79).

32. Giambattista Orsini, Cardinal-Presbyter of the Title of Santa Maria IN DOMNICA.

33. Giangiacomo Sclafenati, Cardinal-Presbyter of the Title of San Stefano AD MONTE CELIO; (*æt.* 32).

VIII. AT THE CONSISTORY OF 1485, Xystus P.M. IIII renounced one cardinal, who was:

34. Ascanio Maria Sforza-Visconti, Cardinal-Δ of Santi Vito e Modesto; (*æt.* 39).*

Analysis will cast these thirty-four creatures of Xystus into three classes:

(*a*) Those of whom a description is given, but not the age.

(*b*) Those of whom no description is given, nor the age.

(*c*) Those whose age at date of creation is given.

Class *a* will be seen to contain sundry clerks, who obviously were decorated with the galerum vermiculum in reward for distinct achievement as ablegates, archbishops, bishops, abbots; or who subsequently succeeded to the paparchy and wrote their own names in history; or who were foreigners advanced for political reasons. This class includes Nos.2, 4, 7, 9, 10, 11, 12, 18, 19, 20, 23, 24, 25, 26.

* This category is compiled from Ciacconj et Oldoini *Vitae Pont. Rom.* III., 42–88. (Ed. Rom. 1677.)

Class *b* contains two names, Nos.17, 32, to which neither age nor official description is appended. Both of these creations were due to the exigencies of domestic policy. Cardinal Girolamo Basso della Rovere was a Pontifical Nephew, and was adorned with the Sacred Purple in his turn among the other clerical sons of the Pope's sisters. Cardinal Giambattista Orsini was a prince of that mighty Roman baronial House, which, for good or for ill, (generally the latter) always had at least one of its members in the Sacred College. In any case the tongue of calumny is not wagged at these.

Class *c* contains three cardinals aged twenty-three, twenty-five, twenty-seven, (Nos.28, 1, 15); three aged thirty-two, thirty-eight, thirty-nine, (Nos.33, 3, 34); two aged forty-two, forty-five, (Nos. 16, 6); two aged fifty, fifty-one, (Nos.5, 8); two aged sixty-one, sixty-two, (Nos.13, 27); four aged seventy, seventy-one, seventy-seven, seventy-nine, (Nos.29, 19, 30, 31). It also contains two cardinals aged fourteen years and sixteen years respectively (Nos. 21, 22). Cardinal Don Juan de Aragona was a son of King Don Ferrando 1 of Naples. The Royal Houses of Europe always could have their junior scions, the fools of the family, fitted with scarlet hats upon the mere request. Cardinal Rafaele Galeotto Sansoni-Riario was the Pontifical Grand-Nephew. His uncle, Count Girolamo Riario, persuaded his Grand-Uncle, Xystus P.M. IIII, to include the adolescent among the Fathers, in order that he might be used as a tool in the ghastly conspiracy of the Pazzi in 1478, he (Rafaele) being a student of the university of Pisa at that time. It may be observed that neither of these cardinal-deacons was a 'page of the bed-chamber', or a 'son of the barber'.

It will be evident that not one of the cardinals created by Xystus can be identified with the puelli delicati to whom allusion has been made; and so the first and third portions of Stefano Infessura's accusation may be cast into that conluvies which is their proper situation.

But, in the second portion, impudically shrieks this Scribe of the Senate and Roman People, why did Xystus show favour to 'comitem Hieronimum, et fratrem Petrum, eius germanum, ac post cardinalem Stĩ Xysti, nisi propter sodomiam?' If Stefano Infessura did not know, at the time when he wrote those odious words in his journal, he will know now, after a sojourn of four hundred years and more in Another Place. Count Girolamo and his brother Pietro were not suitable. They were adult men, and not puerculi. In no sense can they be classed among the παίγνια of whom Stefano Infessura invidiously raved. Count Girolamo Riario was a ruffianly brigand of the age of thirty years, husband of Madonna Catarina Sforza-Visconti. He was of a hybrist imperious habit; and it is notorious that whatever favours, in the way of fiefs or ducats, he obtained from his uncle the Pontiff (Who really wanted to love him but was repelled by his hyperenoreontose manners), were obtained by means of something not unlike intimidation. His brother, Pietro Riario, was a learned and very ambitious Franciscan friar of an equally disagreeable character, who had studied at Venice (where he subsequently occupied the chair of philosophy), Padua, Bologna, Perugia, Siena, and Ferrara. He was Minister-General* of the Religion of St Francis of Assisi for the province of Rome; and he had been prefect of the cell to his Uncle at the latter's election to the pontifical throne in the Conclave of 1471. He already was twenty-five years old, (which means more in Italy than in England, and meant a very great deal more in Italy of the Fifteenth Century even than in Italy of the Twentieth); and, that his Uncle, having heard the momentous words addressed to Himself as the formula of His incoronation, *Accipe tiaram, tribus coronis ornatum, et scias Te esse Patrem principum et regum, Rectorem orbis, in terra Vicarium Salvatoris nostri Jesus Christi*, immediately should proceed to adorn His nephew and former chaplain with the Title of San Sisto, the Patriarchy of Constantinople, and the Archbishopric of Florence, is a perfectly natural and usual piece of nepotism, of course perfectly indefensible, but altogether untainted by Stefano Infessura's akathartic insinuation.

There remains the 'valet' created by John Addington Symonds, the 'lad of no education and of base birth', whose 'merit was the beauty of a young Olympian', who was nominated 'Cardinal and Bishop of Parma at the age of twenty in 1463'. It is not possible to say why he is called a 'lad', if he were twenty years old: for the word inaccurately is applied to a male human animal after his seventeenth year. It is not possible to say why the peculiar epithet of the Diespiter so loosely is applied to him: though certainly the

---

* In the Religion of St Francis, the higher the rank the more servile is the title, 'Whosoever will be great among you let him be your minister; and whosoever will be chief among you let him be your servant,' (St. Matt. xx. 26, 27) is observed to the letter.

comic writers applied it to Perikles. Neither is it possible to identify him with Stefano Infessura's 'pages of the bed-chamber', a situation which his age 'of twenty years' would render improbable. But it is possible to say that, (in theory), 'base birth' does not count against a man in the One Holy Catholic and Apostolic Roman Church, whose first paparch was a plebeian fisherman. And it is possible to say that the mollific suggestion, ingeniously detached from proof, which underlies the statement 'his merit was the beauty of a young Olympian' is inadmissible as a serious contribution to history. And also, to the confusion of John Addington Symonds, it is possible to affirm that Xystus P.M. IIII created no 'cardinal' at all, preconised no 'Bishop of Parma' at all, 'in 1463' (*Renaissance in Italy*, I. 327), for the astounding reason that that Pontiff did not begin to reign until eight years later in 1471.

Throughout the stupendous work from which this calumny (i.e., false as distinct from true slander) is taken, John Addington Symonds has shown an agile ineptitude for recording gossip in preference to fact: although it must be admitted that, in cases where the facts possess more elements of probability than the fictions of professional squibbers, libellers, and lampoonists, he introduces the said fact in a reluctant foot-note, invariably to the entire confutation of the fictions in his text, e.g., the death of Alexander P.M. VI (I. 365) and the death of Lorenzo de Medici (I. 457). But, in the present case, no foot-note confutes gratuitous calumny.

And yet, when naked truth is the object of the historian, this 'cardinal and bishop of Parma' so very easily is identified; and, with his identification, comes complete exposure of the malice (or imbecility) of the disgraceful accusation. The sober fact is that it was Giangiacomo Sclafenati of Milan, who was preconised Bishop of Parma, and pronounced Cardinal-Presbyter of the title of San Stefano *Ad Monte Celio*, by Xystus P.M. IIII, not in 1463, but in the Seventh Creation of 1483. There is no record of his having been a 'valet'. He was a pontifical chamberlain (cubicularius), holding a minor office exactly similar to that held at the date of writing by Monsignor Hartwell de la Garde Grissell, M.A., of Brasenose College, Oxford, whose official style is given on his bookplate as *Cubicularius honoris decurialis ab ense et lacerna Pontificis Maximi*, and whom no one would dream of denominating the 'valet' of Leo P.M. XIII. Nor is there any record of Cardinal Sclafenati's 'base birth'. Ciacconius says 'ex humili' (which only malice or imbecility would render 'base'): but Oldoinus cites numerous authorities who say 'ex nobili genere'; and indeed the name Sclafenati is a gentle name, and might be a noble plural, (cf. Savelli, Lancellotti, Medici, Orsini, Cesarini, Cenci, Sanseverini, Cajetani, Visconti, Manfredi, &c.,) and even the indication of honourable (because legitimatized) bastardy, the preposition 'di' preceding the paternal full-name (e.g., Giangiacomo di Francesco Sclafenati, cf. Tommaso di Cristoforo Fini*) is absent altogether. Further, as may be perceived in the following record of his death, Cardinal Sclafenati was not a 'lad [*sic*] of twenty' but a man of thirty-two, at the date of his creation, and owed his elevation to other and nobler natural gifts than the mere corporeal. An inchanting little picture of him subconsciously is given in his inchanting epitaph, the work of his affectionate brother Madonno Filippo Sclafenati, Knight of the Order of St John of Jerusalem of Malta. It is a miniature, unique, and precious as an intaglio, which needed no re-cutting at the hands of John Addington Symonds:

CHR.   ✠   SAL.

JO. JACOBO SCLAFENATO MEDIOLAN. DIVI STEPHANI IN COELIO S.R.E. PRESBYTERO CARDINALI PARMEN. AB INGENIUM FIDEM SOLERTIAM CAETERAS ANIMI ET CORPORIS DOTES À XYSTO IIII PONT. MAX. INTER PATRES RELATO AC FORTUNIS UNDECUMQUE ORNATO QUEIS PERPETUA MODESTIA INCOMPARABILIQUE INTEGRITATE GNARITER ANNOS XIIII FUNCTO. PHILIPPUS EQ. ORD. HIER. FRATRICŌCORDISS. NATO IIII IDUS SEPT. MCCCCLI MORTUO VI IDUS DECEMBR. MIIID. MOERENS B.M. POSUIT.

The suggestion is pretended that this particular accusation, when it is not accompanied by proofs susceptible of the severest and most stringent cognition, logically should reflect more shame on the accuser than on the accused. It is too periculous a weapon to be used casually, or in idle sport. Its miasma is too deadly to be spread abroad at random. The plea of carelessness, wanton or deliberate, is invalid; and may not be urged to excuse the serious writer of history, whose craft is an Exact Science, in which certain few things are known for certain reasons, and can be placed in the category of facts, certain other things partly are known, and can be

---

* This painter is vulgarly known by his nickname Masolino = Pretty Tommy.

stated under the head of probabilities, while the huge majority of things remain unknown because untested or undiscovered. It is maintained that the writer of history must be content to have his general credibility, his bona fides, gauged by this standard: that, *if he make this charge, he either must drive it home, or must accept the suspicion of having been actuated by malicious intent or by natural bias*; and malice and bias are disqualifications in an historian.

In view of the extreme inaccuracy of Stefano Infessura and John Addington Symonds in the present case of Xystus P.M. IIII, it is claimed that these writers have deserved to have their bona fides doubted, and their respective histories subjected to minute corroboration by such credible authorities as those adumbrated at the beginning of this essay, before they can be included among reliable and veridical (because conscientious) historians.

And, if this predicament be assigned to Stefano Infessura and John Addington Symonds in the case of Xystus P.M. IIII, it also must be assigned to Giangiovio Pontano* in the case of Sigismondo Malatesta and his own son Roberto; to Andrea Dati† in the case of Canon Angelo Ambrogini (called Poliziano) and Giovanni and Giulio de' Medici, with reference to the verses Ἐρωτικὸν Δωριστί, Ἐρωτικὸν, περὶ τοῦ χρυσοκόμου, Εἰς τὸν παῖδα;‡ to Francesco Guicciardini§ in the case of the Borgia and Astorgio

---

* Opera. Venetiis in aedibus Aldi, mdxviii. *De Immanitate quae versatur circa veneream voluptatem.*

† Cited in *Menagiana* IIII. 122. (His poems were printed in Florence in 1546 in 8°.)

‡ These verses are contained in a subrare book called *Carmina Quinque Illustrium Poetarum*, published at Bergamo in 1753, and adorned with the following definite Imprimatur:

'Noi Riformatori dello Studio di Padova. Avendo veduto per la Fede di revisione ed approvazione del P.F.Andrea Bonfadio Inquisitor-Generale del S. Offizio di Bergamo nel Libro intitolato *Carmina Quinque Illustrium Poetarum, Petri Bembi, Andreae Naugerj, Balthassaris Castiglionj, Joannis Casae, et Angeli Politiani; additis Jacobi Sadoleti, S.R.E.Cardinalis Carminibus; Joannis Baptistae Amaltei quinque selectissimus Eclogis; Benedicti Lampridj et M.Antonj Flaminj ineditis quibusdam; etc.*; non v' esser cos' alcuna contra la S.Fede Cattolica; e parimente per attestato del Segretario Nostro, niente contro Prencipi, e buoni costumi; concediamo Licenza a *Pietro Lancelotti Stampatore di Bergamo*, che possa essere stampato, osservando gli ordini in materia di stampe, e presentando le solite copie alle Publiche Librerie di Venezia e di Padova.

'Dat. li 17 Maggio 1753.   (Gio. Emo. Proc. Rif.
                              (Barbon, Morosini Cav. Proc. Rif.
                              (Alvise Mocenigo 4. Cav. Proc. Rif.

'Registrato in Libro a C. ii. al n. 68.   Gio. Girolamo Zuccato. Segr.'
§ L'historia d'Italia. Ed. Mil. v., 26.

and Gianevanglista Manfredi; to Benedetto Varchi* in the case of Duke Pierluigi Farnese of Parma and Bishop Cosimo Gueri da Pistoja of Fano; and also it must be assigned to all writers who, in any age, have followed their example. *The charge*, when made, *must be proved to the uttermost*, by direct and positive as distinct from circumstantial evidence, *on pain of the accuser*. *The unproved suspicion*, assiduously disseminated by the venomous tongue of man, of woman or of clerk, assiduously tabulated by the venomous pen of scribes like Stefano Infessura and John Addington Symonds, must be regarded solely as an emanation of a kopriematose imagination, and *should be made to recoil upon its own inventor or disseminator* with everlasting shame. Genius and rank, for centuries, have been the victims of a handful of ordurous journalistic mediocrities, whom modern writers contentedly follow because they are antique and remote. It is for the Twentieth Century to devise some test, some standard, whereby a certain approximation to historical truth may become attainable. The criterion, which herein has been adopted, in all humility is pretended for examination.

* Storia Fiorentina. Ed. Mil. xvi., xvii.

The Venetians

I am consumed by a blazing desire to know precisely what the clergy of Venice, and what the fathers of families in Venice, have been doing during the last few (let us say five) centuries. One thing I think I know which the former certainly have omitted to do – they do not seem ever to have shaved, excepting with old and blunted scissors, and rarely, even so. The spectacle, indeed, which Their Reverences and Very Reverences present, is so indescribably frowsy and disgusting, that pure piety has caused me to vow a donation of a thousand Autostrop Safety Razors, with the relative soap and brushes, to the Cardinal-Patriarch of Venice, for distribution among and compulsory use by His clergy, immediately on my earning ten thousand pounds by means of one of my books. But, joking apart – though I'm quite serious about the razors – I cannot for the life of me imagine how the spiritual and temporal fathers of Venice have been occupying themselves (apart from their animalistic functions) during several generations. This is why.

I had a thoroughly puritan (but detestable and inefficacious) bringing-up myself, such as I believe my antecessors had before me. We are a typically narrow constricted and entirely insular little family of unadulterated English blood, without the slightest admixture of Erse, Keltic, or any foreign strain for at least the last six generations. Whether it is due to this, or (as I fancy) to the rigorous ideas inherited, or imparted by our spiritual and temporal fathers, I cannot surely say: but of one thing I am quite certain, i.e., that we have certain clear and sharp and fixed notions of Right and Wrong, and certain inevitable principles of Honour and Decency. I don't say that we act up to them: we are men, not gods. But I do fearlessly assert – and I don't care twopence for your yelling 'Pharisee' at me, O most affable reader – that, in this matter, we are 'not as other men are, extortioners, unjust, adulterers, or even as these' Venetians. Of course I (who rejoice to call myself a bigoted Roman Catholic of twenty-eight terrible years' standing) score frightfully by having the Sacred Scriptures, with all their incomparable poetry and their unsurpassable maxims at my fingers' ends. I admit that there I have the advantage over most other miserable mortals, thanks to my puritan up-bringing. But of course also I am fully aware that I formed myself, such as I am, to an enormous and incalculable extent, on the teaching and example of my spiritual pastors and masters, as well as of my parents, and the unconsciously absorbed traditions of my race. And I simply say that I am stupefied, flabbergasted, when I contemplate the results of my five years' study of the Venetians and set out to criticize (chastize) them, in proof of my undying love for them, by means of such standards as I have. I can't go as far as W.D.Howells, who criticized them from his (American) standards, about fifty-forty years ago, and talk about their most shameless ignorance, their most polite corruption, their most unblushing baseness. To me, the Venetians whom I have met, seem to be merely inadequate, incondite, banausic, and perfectly complacent about it.

Of course it's inexpressibly comical. A joke in sober earnest always is. I don't for a moment mean that my Venetians pose (for reasons known only to themselves) as inadequate, incondite, banausic, and complacent. No: they really are all those and desperately serious about it; and I think that is why I find them so loveable and amusing. Certainly I never encountered anyone even remotely like them all my life long. But, after all, when one comes to analyse and ponder these curious phenomena, there does not seem to be anything particularly unnatural in their possession of the qualities which I find in them. They are a mixed race, originally Illyrian, then Romanized, and subsequently adulterated beyond measure with Teutonic and Slovenic and Levantine and Asiatic strains. They were as late as 1866 the bond-slaves of Ostrogoths and Huns and Croats, and are only now in process of formation into Italians under the illuminated sceptre of Savoja, though the commerce and enterprise and society of their city remains even yet largely occupied by Austro-Hungarians and Germans. What, then, can be expected of the Venetians but inadequacy, seeing that not fifty years ago she was barred off from the procession of the nations along the path of modern civilization? Here are a few examples of what I call inadequacy. You must know, O most affable reader, that I always keep a few little wooden idols, from $1\frac{1}{2}$ to 2 feet high, to carve at when my hand gets tired with pen-driving. I can't rest (i.e. remain inactive) ever; and I find that change of manual labour prevents stagnation of energy. Last winter, it chanced that I had got one of my idols into a certain stage of completion: but, the wood being knotty and unequally coloured, I was unable to judge the purity of planes and contours. I therefore painted the idol a uniform ivory-white, and stuck it up to study in leisured intervals of writing; and, the result was a resolution to refine it with further carving here and further filing there and a lot of rubbing with the rough fish-skin which they call *pelle del angelo* all over. But – horror – I could not get the paint off, or the wood bare and fit for cutting with cold steel. And, to me, at the moment, there occurred, by chance, a blond and socialistic artisan with wild blue eyes frequently employed by me for similar odds and ends, to whom I exposed my predicament. He laughed sweetly, saying that it was a mere nothing to one (like him) who knew; and he took my idol away, promising to return it freed from taint of paint on the morrow. I being very much occupied with other things, forgot all about it till a week later, when, one day, returning to my workshop, I had the pleasant surprise of finding my idol on its pedestal – it was Hermes singing for his grandson Odysseys before the areio-pagos of the blessed gods – perfectly clean and beautiful and ready for my knives and files. I confess that I sat contemplating the lovely thing for half-an-hour, planning refinements and promising myself an infinity of poetic pleasures. And to me entered sadly my blue-eyed artisan, timidly creeping, grievous of mien, suffering pathetically, extending bleeding and badly skinned and blistered hands for compassion. And oh, he moaned, was My Sioria contented with my god? Most contented, I replied: but how had he cleaned it so exquisitely? With caustic soda; and, behold the consequence – his hands, with which he gained his living, burnt and scalded and hanging in rags and tatters to the tune of (let us say) L.32. 'But, dear fair male,' I asked, 'were you not previously aware of the corrosive properties of caustic soda?' *Altro che*, but naturally, seeing that he used it every day in his art and mystery. Then, why did he put his hands in it? But how could he have cleaned the paint off my idol – it was well done, wasn't it true? – I had said that I was contented, wasn't it true? – without putting his hands in it. But why, when the first spot of caustic soda caused him to caper, did he persist in imbuing his hands in it? *Macchè!* (with a noble and heroic gesture,) did not his honour oblige him at all sacrifices to content the rich and generous Sior Inglese. I kindly pointed out that I myself would have used balls of rag tied to sticks, and old toothbrushes for the crevices. But he smiled patronisingly. I was an eminent, very eximious, and most clearly illuminating writer, such being my proper art and mystery: but, in the matter of cleaning paint off wooden idols with caustic soda, I was (wasn't it true?) a mere dilettante, whereas he the speaker was a conoscente and the facts remained I was content with my idol and that he was damaged on my account to the extent named. So I paid, and made a note of what I choose here to call inadequacy, – not for want of a juster word, but because I propose to treat the banausic (and more diverting) aspect of my experiences in a place by itself.

Nor do I find the shop-keepers (I mean the sellers of life's necessities, not the almost universal vendors of trumpery manufactured in Birmingham and Germany for sale as Venetian work to tourists) one whit more adequate than the artisan. My grocer, when I complained of the putridity of his last consignment of 23 out of 30 tins of condensed milk, politely accepted my monthly cheque and informed me that he could not guarantee the freshness of his goods and invited me to take my prized custom elsewhere. But I think the best example of a tradesman's inadequacy is the following. I wanted a punching-bag, like Hubert Bland's – one whose base stands on the floor instead of dangling from the door or ceiling. Perhaps I ought to explain that I pay part of my debt to Italy for her hospitality by trying to make trustworthy disciplined athletes of some of her elegant exquisites and other pretentious loafers and puppies. Lord! how they detest me! But I've done it in half a dozen cases, already, as this very year's conscription can testify. Anyhow, I went to Marforio where you buy athletic appliances and demanded a punching-bag. After some search in trade catalogues, they found the desired model, and informed me that it was made in two qualities, the one would cost me L.100, and the other L.125, both including carriage from London and duty paid – they were ready to order both for me to see, if I would guarantee to purchase one. This seemed fair enough and I gave the order, which they promised to execute in a fortnight. After waiting 6 weeks, I told them that I was off to Florence for a week, and, if the punching-bag had not arrived on my return, they might consider the order cancelled, as I didn't like being played with. But, in Florence, I happened by chance to see an English sports catalogue, which informed me that I could have those identical punching-bags for £1.12.6 or £1.19.9 respectively; and of course, on reaching Venice after fifteen days' absence, I found that Marforio was still in default with my order. I therefore wrote him a formal cancellation, on the grounds of his eight weeks' delay and of the actual retail prices of the goods by me fortuitously discovered. His answer was polite information that the punching-bags were now at my disposal. I repeated my cancellation. Up then surged his manager with a sheaf of papers and a wan pathetic look, to prove to me from documents in hand that, though it was perfectly true that the punching-bags at wholesale prices only cost him about thirty-four and forty-two francs each, yet he had had to pay something like sixty and seventy francs each for duty, not to speak of carriage. And behold the papers in proof of it. I blankly beheld them – and mounted in a fury instantly. Why was he inviting me to inspect the Customs' receipts for duty paid on articles made of worked leather? He instantly became extremely lucid and instructive – it was quite true that only an ounce or two of the consignment (namely the binding of the seams of the canvas-bags) was of stitched leather, all the rest of the weight (about a cwt) being of cast iron, cane, and such like base material: but, seeing that it was all packed together in one case, naturally the Customs charged the highest duty possible, namely that on worked leather, lumping the whole bulk together. Here, I confess, I became incapable of uttering civil words: I said severely 'Go away, and I will write to you.' 'My respects to you,' he sweetly gushed, 'I revere you very distinctly.' And he went piously away. Now you must remember, O most affable reader, that I did actually want a punching-bag very badly and immediately, and that I did not want the bother and delay of fighting Marforio and ordering another from England. So I wrote that if an eminent and respectable firm like Marforio would tell me definitely that it was its intention to make me pay L.100 instead of L.40 or L.125 instead of L.60 for its stupid blunder in omitting to tell its London agent to pack the cheap and bulky cast iron apart from the costly and infinitesimal worked leather, I

was willing to take the cheaper punching-bag at the price agreed
and I enclosed a cheque on the Banca Veneta worth L.100. And
that brought Marforio in person, raving, and threatening to bring
a legal *querela* against me for outrage on his honour with the words
stupid and blunder in writing which he himself published to all and
sundry. The scene took place at high noon in the hall of the pub
where I feed. As the Venetian manner is, all sorts of the usual loafers
sprang excitedly to hear Marforio and to see the conflict. Sedulous
waiters begged me, lying low and laughing at my lunch within, to
gush out and interview him. I asked for the salt. An alarmed
manager with pacific intentions slid in and whispered. Did I know
that M. was telling the proprietors of the pub that I had called him
stupid. Wouldn't I consent to tell M. that I didn't understand
Italian, that 'stupid' in English meant something quite different
and harmless and that every English called every other English
stupid every day without rancour or bloody war. No I wouldn't do
anything of the sort. But, indeed, Marforio was *arrabbiatissimo*, and
would certainly drag me before the tribunal. Here, my notorious
and more than Jobian patience gave way with a loud bang, as
follows. 'Please,' I said, 'go away; and tell the inestimable Marforio,
that I never write a letter excepting for publication, that he himself
published the letter in which I didn't call him stupid except hypo-
thetically, that he can publish it as much as he dam pleases, in the
lawcourts and the journals, that he holds my cheque, and that if the
punching-bag isn't in my house and the cheque cashed and the
incident closed by 15 o'clock (it's now 13) today, I'll go to the bank
and stop the cheque and all other wise harry and defy him. But I
withdraw nothing except my previous opinion of his business-like
adequacy.' The manager moaned: but the punching-bag was
delivered with obsequious and smiling promptitude, and the
cheque was cashed within the hour, and I never had any more
dealings pleasant or unpleasant with Marforio.

I could go on with these instances of bourgeois incompetency
for a fortnight. The case of the eximious Sig. Enea Drog, who (out
of sincere admiration, disinterested friendship, pure love, and all
that sort of rot) butted himself forward to make me working
designs of the antique bragozzo in the Arsenal Museum, with an
arched-roofed cabin between the fore and main masts to meet my
needs, which designs could be used for building me a practicable

10-metre bragozzo by the ship builders of vicinal Chioggia, was
of a comicality which makes me laugh *a sbellicarmi, a metter a novo
un cristiano* even now. Pious Enea, a hypochondriacal jack of all
trades, – clerk of the works, taxidermist, sculptor, artist (religious
and portrait), and born Venetian, were a few of the mysteries
practised by him, shewed himself most perfectly incapable of
absorbing my ideas and wishes, reducing them to practical form,
and giving me what I wanted. I had an exact copy of the antique
bragozzo made, and personally added to it the modifications which
I desired to have. You must clearly understand, O most affable
reader, that I have actually been homeless and penniless and
starving and friendless, so many times in my life – ten times at the
very least, and certainly three times during the last $5\frac{1}{2}$ years here
in Venice – that knowing (as Cassiodorus says) that 'the sea is a
refuge in time of danger' and that the death which comes by water
is the gentlest death (and the loveliest) that may be, I am unalter-
ably determined at all times and in all circumstance to have and
to hold a strong little ship, manageable by me, beautiful because
simple and capable, commodious to live and labour in, as a refuge
in time of danger, i.e. as a retreat where never again I shall experience the unspeakable horrors of being looked at by pietose philan-
thropists while I writhe in my death-agonies. I had thought it all
out carefully and knew precisely what I wanted: but Enea was so
saturated with his own notions of what sort of elegant pleasure craft
an eccentric and rich (oh but rich of a richness!) English *miliardario*
ought to want, that he – well, I merely say that he tired me. The
making of the working designs spread over weeks and months, the
ship grew from 10 to 15 metres in length which meant that I should
neither be able to row nor to sail the monster by myself and that my
deliberate choice of privacy would be violated. Finally, when the
Drog told me (with screams and capers and gesticulations) that if
I had an arched-roofed cabin I should look like a flat-roofed piroga
of the dazio and that so I mustn't have a cabin at all and when his
chorus – a chorus invariably collects round a Venetian who begins
to dictate to a foreigner – echoed him and stared at me sardonically,
I gently wiped the lot of them, wiping them as a man (wiping a dish)
wipeth it and turneth it upside down.

Of the adequacy or inadequacy of professional classes in Venice,
i.e. the Church, Navy, Army and Law, I am not highly competent

to offer criticism. I know little or nothing of their reverences the autokthonous clergy for reasons which perhaps may be understood. I find (so far in life) the Faith comfortable and the faithful intolerable. I use the holy men as ministers of means of grace: but they always try to be magisterial and neglect their razors. Consequentially I personally know none of them. My parish priest sent me notice last Holy Saturday that he was coming to bless my house at 14 o'clock. I sent him word that he would be welcomed to perform his function and afforded every facility by my factor, and regretted that I myself would be absent, it not being my custom to make the personal acquaintance of the clergy, for the simple reason that as a tonsured clerk who for 26 years had not ceased to assert a denied divine vocation for the priesthood, I was *persona ingrata* to the clergy who knew me and had no intention of adding new ones to that number. I then put a bank-note in an envelope addressed to my parish priest, which I left with my factor for handing to his reverence as *honorarium* for the Rite of Easter benediction; and betook myself to lunch at a fourteenth-century pub called the Cavalletto at 13 o'clock and to stroll in Piazza till 16 o'clock. Oh – well – his reverence never came. I kept the valuable envelope till Pentecost and then sent it to him by registered post, for his poor, with a note politely regretting that he had been unable to do his Easter duty. He assured me by letter that he would pray for me, and pouched the bank-note, and leaves my house unblessed – but whether this is adequacy or inadequacy, I prefer not to attempt to say.

Venetians who make things don't seem any more capable and adequate either. I wanted a rather large waterproof tarpaulin to cover the topo in which I lived while I wrote *The Weird of the Wanderer* and *Hubert's Arthur*. Venice is not all opalescent sunbeams: violent storms of wind and rain often make the lagoon a horror, and the vicissitudes of those two books since I began to write them in 1907 were of a horror which firmly resolved me not to take any more risks of damage (either from thieves or weather) to my final copies (the sixth and ninth respectively) of the MSS. I was advised that Spiridion was the man to make my awning and I got him down to the boat one day, described precisely the kind and shape of tarpaulin which I needed, furnished him with drawings of it, shewed him a pattern of the canvas which I in-

tended to buy for him to cut and sew, and made him personally
measure the arched wooden framework, to be roofed in by the
tarpaulin (which was to cover me when I slept at night and when
I drove my pen in inclement weather) and to tell me how much
of the chosen canvas he needed. He said twenty metres, length at
L.7 the metre and I promised the thing within the week. It was to
cost me L.60 for making up. I gave him the canvas and the wooden
framework, and as he had a little marine store, I took some rope
and a canvas bucket and a little folding anchor of him to be paid
for with the work which he had in hand. And I waited four weeks,
which mercifully were all sunshiny so that my work went ahead
without let or hindrance, before the dear man delivered my twenty
metres of stuff made up into a beautiful tarpaulin which covered
all but precisely nineteen inches at the end of my framework just
over where my head would be. Imagine a builder who delivered a
house minus nineteen inches of roof, O most affable reader; and
you will understand my ravings to the address of Spiridion. He
said that the canvas had shrunk, that it hurt his fingers to sew it,
and that he felt tired of it. I said that he had wasted my canvas
(L.140) because you must make your tarpaulins longways and to
join another nineteen inches crossways would prevent my roof from
being perfectly waterproof and spoil its beauty as well. He said, as
Venetians do when cornered, that he didn't know nothing about
nothing properly nothing. I therefore threw the spoiled canvas and
wooden framework at him on his doorstep (literally), told him
that I should keep the other goods I had had of him to repay my
loss, and so left him, while I went and had some light iron rods and
arches made, easily fixable when necessary, bought another lot of
canvas which I cut to shape myself and got an old sailor to sew
the hems and joins. This served me perfectly and I heard nothing
of inadequate Spiridion for 18 months. He wanted full payment
for his inadequacy and (specially) he wanted his little anchor
which he said was a priceless patent model. It was actually a very
common oldfashioned thing, but I imagine he had got a chance of
selling it to some member of the new Venetian Yacht Club just then
started to offend the aesthetic of the lagoon with modern crafts,
deemed smart and of a chic, and here called 'coot-airs'. (I think
they mean cutters, but they are German anyhow.) I merely re-
marked that he had had L.140 of my canvas (spoiled by him) for a

year and a half and that I wasn't going to pay him the 10th of a penny or to give up the anchor. He went to the Delegate, a curious kind of police magistrate who decides whether you're guilty or not in his private office after hearing the complaint against you. This particular functionary happened to be a Neapolitan dressed in a little brief authority: he summoned me to the Questura and proceeded nasally to bully the rich foreigner (!). I listened serenely to my condemnation to pay Spiridion about L.130 and to return his priceless patent model anchor on pain of being hauled up before the Praetor; and, as serenely, but perhaps a little vividly, informed the Delegate that I would consider carefully what he had been so graciously illuminating as to say, and communicate my decision to him on the following day. Then I went home and prepared everything for sinking the anchor irretrievably in 30 feet of water at a quiet part of the Canale del Orfano between San Servolo and San Clemente, being determined that if I couldn't have it neither should the wretched blunderer and extortioner: after which, I wrote to the Delegate formally saying that I was ready to pay the inadequate Spiridion his L.130, and to return his priceless patent model anchor after receiving from him my L.140 worth of waterproof canvas in good condition which he had held for 18 months, and after he had proved by exhibition of the patent that the anchor really was a patent model and priceless. And I have never heard another word on this subject or any other from Spiridion: though people (quite unknown to me) from his neighbourhood used to pop up here there and everywhere for a month or two saying that I owed them small sums like L.30 or L.40, to all of whom I said sweetly, 'I pray you to communicate with me through the Lord Delegate Cuocolo'; and they also blenched suddenly and withered away.

Concerning England and Germany

With regard to Germany and the Germans, how would it be to try a different point of view?

It is the fashion for England to look askance at Germany, as a successful competitor, a possible rival, a likely-to-be-dangerous enemy, but (anyhow) as an example to be imitated. Pseud-empirics on all sides aver (with shouts) that things are done better in Germany: that labour is cheaper, wages higher, output of produce superior in quality and quantity, conditions of life more comfortable, state-service more efficient and more economical, sanitary arrangements more perfect – Mr Frank Bullen (for example) preaches that the English mercantile marine would be well-advised to take Teutonic tips: while Lord Northcliffe, the ochlokratic hysteriarch of the *Dylymyle*, would have English coal-miners to ape the German.

That is the present English view-point.

Far be it from me to blast it with unconditional anathema. I merely suggest that peradventure there may be another, from which a more accurate conspectus of the situation might be obtained. All experience shews that the mass of mankind never judges for itself, never sees anything clearly until it has been told. Please, therefore, let me do a little telling – the merest sketch of a tale.

Now, while a nation's character is formed by its circumstances, its own desire (to mould it in a particular way) is one of those circumstances, and by no means one of the least important. Well then: is it England's desire to take Germany for a model? If so, why? If not, why not?

How would it be for England to come off the peak, from which She at present regards Germany as a Young Vigorous Something On The Way Up: and to climb to the point (scientifically known as *The Doctrine of Philosophical Necessity* – the short cut is by way of *Historical Inevitability* –) whence Germany at once becomes plainly visible as a Senile Exhausted Something Tottering Along The Way Down?

A word in explanation. The *Doctrine of Philosophical Necessity* is briefly this: Given the motives present in a nation's mind, and given also the character and disposition of the said nation, the manner in which it will act may be unerringly inferred. If we know the nation thoroughly, and all the inducements which are acting on it, we can foretell its conduct with as much certainty as we can predict any physical event.

This being so, we will take a look at our history-books. It's plain, from them, that a nation is a magnified man. Macrocosm equals Microcosm, in everything but size. A nation goes through boyhood, adolescence, youth, manhood, seniority, old age, just as a man does. Then it dies: leaving (or not leaving) progeny, just like a man. Need I more than mutter Egypt, Assyria, Greece, Rome? The bare names suffice. Then, threescore years and ten is supposed (on quite respectable authority) to be the average life of man. Let us put the average life of a nation at thirty times that. The scale is exaggerated: but it may serve.

This being granted, it follows that Germany was a strong healthy well-grown boy in the First Century before and the First Century after Christ. Anyone can read all about this in Caesar's *Gallic War*, and Tacitus's *Manners and Peoples of Germany*. At the opening of the Ninth Century, in AD 800, Charles the Great being emperor, it's not unfair to say that Germany was in the full flower of glory-loving youth, passing into manhood's magnificence under the Hottos, and the Henrys, and the Conrads, until Frederick Red-Beard died in the Twelfth Century.

That sums a thousand years of ever-increasing vigour. Follow, a hundred years, when German sovereigns regularly marched to Rome (by roads lined with burnt cities and paved with corpses,) for imperial incoronation; and yet another hundred years, in which they, not only did all these things but also, selected and nominated and confirmed God's Vicegerents, 'the Rulers of the world, the Fathers of princes and kings, the Earthly Vicars of Jesus Christ our Saviour', Whom they forced to crown them. The Roman Paparchy actually was in the German Emperor's pocket. How's that for a nation's manhood and seniority?

In old age, four hundred years later, Germany was still hale under Charles the Fifth. And, marvellous to relate, even in extreme senility, Dr Bismarck's blood and iron tonic keeps life in the old bones, under really and truly as fine a specimen of an emperor as the world has seen – Caesar Guilhelmus Secundus Imperator Augustus.

Have I sketched the skeleton of an idea?

Do I hear some pessimist idiot say that what I allege of Germany equally applies to England – that, if Germany is on the facile descent, England indubitably is too?

What ineffable nonsense! Let us turn to the history-books again.

In Germany's boyhood, this island was infested with naked little Keltic barbarians, painted blue and inarticulately howling; and there was no England at all. England was not even born, till the landing of the English in A D 449. Alfred the Great nursed the infant in the Ninth Century. William the Conqueror chastised England's boyhood in the Eleventh Century. When Frederick Red-Beard died in A D 1190, England was coming to puberty under the Plantagenets. Tudors and Stewarts educated England's lusty adolescence. The Divine Victoria superintended the last stage of England's priggish youth. And Edward the Excellent's master-hand touched up England's majority and gave it a shove off to fend for itself.

And now, England is standing on the aretic threshold of manhood; and what (in the Name of Goodness) are Englishmen going to do? Feebly ignore and shirk their proper potentiality, and meekly and meanly ape decrepit superannuated climacteric dotage? Or to themselves be true?

Three Book Reviews

Flipperty Gibberty France

In Literature, the French Reaction began in the name of Sentiment with Madame de Staël and her literary followers. In Society it began in the name of Order with Robespierre and his revolutionary adherents. They were Rousseau's pupils. After the reaction against Voltaire came the reaction against Rousseau; after the festival of the Supreme Being came the Te Deum in Notre-Dame; after Madame de Staël came the Vicomte de Bonald. The principle of sentiment was ousted, or employed (e.g. by Chateaubriand) to support Authority – i.e. the principle which assumes individual and national life to be based on reverence for inherited tradition. The principle of Order was merged in that of Authority, which controlled every domain of life and literature. The Supernatural everywhere supplanted the Natural. Soon it became evident that the principle of the new matter – i.e. Christian tradition – was at utter variance with the traditional principles of literature. In turn, Authority itself began to totter. Beneath the doctrine of the supremacy of universal reason, as set forth by Félicité de la Mennais, the most consistent and determined expositor and defender of Authority, was seen the revolutionary doctrine of the supremacy of the democracy. Thus Authority became *felo de se*. The foes of the liberty of the Press became compelled in self-defence to use that very liberty. The foes of parliamentary government became compelled to defend it, in order to defeat a Ministry which kept them in opposition. All the personages who began by championing Authority and its representatives ended in bitter antagonism to both.

This is Dr Georg Brandes' thesis in the third set of his scholarly series;* and, granting the sufficiency and validity of his premises, we admit that he reaches his conclusion with ingenuity and élan.

* *Main Currents in Nineteenth Century Literature, Vol. III: The Reaction in France.* By Georg Brandes. – Ed.

His sketches of the glucose Chateaubriand, with his pious, mysterious romanticism – of the versatile De Maistre, defender of ideal slaughter and the Inquisition, whose Christianity was 'fear, passive obedience, and State religion' – of De Bonald, the monotonous mediæval schoolmaster – of the susceptible enthusiast, Mme de Krüdener, the adulterous author of 'truly delicious' love stories with pious morals, who was converted by a 'happy' cobbler to the Moravian heresy – of the Jesuits, those ridiculous mediocrities, always pitifully burrowing, burrowing, like assiduous moles, always suffering the sight of pains mis-spent and of elaborate schemes ruined except when quite by accident they chance to kill a king – of Lamartine, the vapid lyrical dilettante – of Victor Hugo, the giant genius – of La Mennais, the apostate, who failed to see with Boccaccio's Jew that a Christianity which could survive amid the infamies of Christians must be divine – and of all who first built up and then threw down again the fallen power Authority – are brilliant and (as far as they go) convincing. Dr Brandes' own standpoint is that of prosecutor. He cites all these witnesses in proof of his contention that 'the principle (Authority) falls never to rise again'. Certainly he clearly shows that it fell in France in the nineteenth century. But 'never'? Is it safe to deduce an Universal from the example of a single century in a single country the characteristics of whose people are, as they were in Cæsar's day, alacrity, utter inability to resist calamity, mobility, and the insatiable habit of seeking novelty. Ought not a more comprehensive field of history to have been examined? Ought not the intermittent vagaries of human nature to be taken into account? Must not the kathekasta be exhausted before the katholoy can be discovered? In short, is it not confounding universals with particulars to denounce the Faith, which is comfortable, simply because the Faithful happen to be intolerable?

A Scented Garden

Professor Browne's Prolegomena to Persian Literature (for that is the apter title for his latest book*) is just one of those rare bright generous illuminants which enable us to realise and know the truth of the Persian axiom, 'Man is a little world, and the world is a

* *A Literary History of Persia from the Earliest Times until Firdawsi.* By E. G. Browne. – Ed.

magnified man.' He has not addressed himself to that futile fetich of illiterate publishers, the 'Library Public', whose horizon is bounded by the *Gulistán* of Sa'dí, the *Díwán* of Háfidh and the so-called *Quatrains* of Edward FitzGerald. Nor will be found in his pages anecdotes of Hárúnu'r-Rashíd's nocturnal rambles through the streets of Bagdad in the company of Ja'far the Barmecide and Masrúr the black executioner, familiar to readers of the *1001 Nights*. But rather does he seek to interest, not the professional Orientalist, but that growing body of amateurs who, having learned to love the Persian poets in tralations, desire to know more of the language, literature, history, and thought of one of the most ancient, gifted, and original peoples in the world.

Now the thought of Persia cannot be known without a wide acquaintance with Arabic, any more than the motives and conduct of a Scots Covenanter or an English Puritan, or even Milton's verse, can be understood without an intimate knowledge of the Bible. On this point Professor Browne repeatedly lays stress. 'Without a knowledge of the Arabic language and literature,' says he, 'one never could hope to be more than a smatterer in Persian.' And again: 'It would seem that Arabic must have been as well understood in Persia by persons of education as English is in Wales at the present time, and that there were eloquent Persians then who could wield the Arabic language as skilfully as several Welsh orators can the English in this our day.' And if the mental process of Persian literates be difficult to master by reason of linguistic difficulties, no less recondite and hard to be understood is that particular species of religious standpoint which informs all Persian thought. To us faith and righteousness are essentials; to the Persians knowledge and mystery. Here religion is regarded as a rule whereby to live and a hope wherein to die; there, as a key to unlock the secrets of the spiritual and material universe. Here a creed is admired for its simplicity; there for its complexity. And with these preliminaries we thankfully enough take the 'Sir Thomas Adams' Professor of Arabic and sometime Lecturer in Persian in the University of Cambridge' as our cicerone in the new world of men and letters opened to us in these 521 demy octavo pages.

And what a world it is! – a new strange world perfumed with musk and ambergris; a world of poetical ætiology, where the 'pallor' of the gold dínár is ascribed to that coin's terror of lavish and prodigal hands; a world of inscriptions and documents of ancient Persia, of pre-Muhammedan literature; of legendary histories set forth in the book of Achæmenian kings; of authentic histories of the Sásánian Period (AD 226–652), of the Arab Invasion, of the Umayyad Period (AD 661–749), of the Early 'Abbásid Period or Golden Age of Islám (AD 749–847), of the Great Persian Heresiarchs, of the feuds of Sunníte and Shí'ite, of Isma'ílís and Carmathians, of the Súfí Mysticism, of the First Period of the Decline of the Califate (AD 850–1000); a world of letters 'full of tropes, similes, metaphors, innuendos, hyperboles, antitheses, quotations, ætiologies, amphibologies, homonomies, anagrams'; a world of men of letters who wrote deliciously, deliriously, not for the general public, but for patrons on whom they depended for a living; for which cause many of them, like 'Unsurí, Farrukhí, Khágání, Dhanír of Fáryáb, whom the Persians reckon among their greatest, never, when tralated, can appeal to Europeans, 'whose sympathies rather will be won by the epic, lyric, didactic, mystic, satirist or pessimist poets like Firdawsí, Háfidh, Sa'di, Násir-i-Khusraw, Jelálu'd-Dín Rúmí, and 'Umar Khayyám, each of whom in a different way appeals to some ground common to all mankind'.

Through this scented garden-world we wander, lingering from time to time to marvel at a profundity of passionate piety (which would be singular in a modern Jesuit like St Francis Xavier – whom we do not accuse of literary plagiarism on account of his hymn, 'My God, I love Thee not because I hope for Heaven thereby') – as instanced in the aphorism of the saintly woman Rábi'a al-'Adawiyya (AD 752):

O God! If I worship Thee for fear of Hell, send me to Hell; and, if I worship Thee from hopes of Paradise, withhold Paradise from me; but, if I worship Thee for Thine Own Sake, then withhold not from me the Eternal Beauty (p. 426),

or we hearken to the wailing lover's lamentation of Qábús v. Washmgír, prince of Tabaristán (AD 976–1012):

> Six things there be that have their home
> In the midst of thy raven hair;
> Twist and tangle, curl and knot,
> Ringlet and lovelock fair:
> Six things there be, as thou mayst see,

Which in mine heart do reign;
Grief and desire, and sorrow dire,
Longing, and passion, and pain. (p. 471.)

Or we ponder the curiously familiar philososphy of the ode of Shams-i-Tabríz:

Poor copies out of Heaven's original,
Pale earthly pictures mouldering to decay,
What care though all your beauties break and fall,
When that which gave them life endures to aye. (p. 440.)

Or we vibrate to the inciting clarion of Handhala of Bádghís (AD 820–872):

If lordship lie within the lion's jaws,
Go, risk it, and from those dread portals seize
Such straight-confronting death as men desire –
Or riches, greatness, rank, and lasting ease. (p. 355.)

And among the vermeil blossoms of the Persian garden we encounter Personages – Zoroaster and his 'Most Luminous Religion', the Prophet Muhammad with his 'rhymed prose Qur'án', al-Muqanna' the Veiled Prophet of Khurásán (and 'Lalla Rookh'), and Khusraw Parwíz, and Darius the Mede, and Cyrus the Elder, and Alexander the Great Conquistator, and 'Ali and al-Hasan and al-Husayn the Martyrs, to say nothing of the Caliph al Mansúr, and an innumerable multitude of writers and singers and sots and sophists and cynics and sinners and saints – in sooth a goodly company.

To return to the book. We do not think that Professor Browne has made enough of the violet-odorous influence of Hellas upon Írán; and we are not quite sure that we go all the way with him (citing Mr Stanley Lane-Poole's *Muhammadan Dynasties*) in deriving both the Shi'ite Imáms and the Fátimid Caliphs from 'Alí; and we strongly object to 'dresst' and 'oppresst' in the English translation from Shahíd of Balkh on p. 454. Yet we have nothing but admiration for the marvellous dexterity and the expository candour which he has brought to this enormous and intricate achievement – and achievement is the apt word here – for his work is in fact an example of concise arrangement combined with opulent discursion, manœuvred with discretion, and consolidated by perfectly amazing erudition. A bibliography and index are appended convenient to the purpose for which they are pretended. We eagerly look for the second volume (promised in the preface), the *History of Persian Literature in the Strict Meaning of the Term*. We say that we look eagerly, for, as the Persian poet cited by Professor Browne on p. 90 says,

> The man of parts who after wisdom strives
> Should have on earth at least a brace of lives;
> In one, experience he then might learn;
> And in the next, that same to profit turn.

Tennyson in Mist

Sir Alfred Lyall's record stands to assure us that he knows his India; but in his newly-published Life of Tennyson* we have been unable to find a single feature which would qualify him to rank as an exponent of Tennyson, the English Man of Letters. Not that it is erroneous in fact; not that it is written ungrammatically; not that it is difficult or ungrateful to read (though the punctuation is the punctuation of the printers' devil); not even that it is deformed by Br Roger Bacon's Four Stumbling-blocks to Truth, except, perhaps, the Imperfections of Undisciplined Senses, or by Francis Bacon's Four Sources of Error, except, perhaps, the Individual Idiosyncrasies, Idols of the Den. But it is trite. But it is amorphose. But it is unilluminating. It leaves the personality of Tennyson indistinct. It leaves the tale of the best work of his transcendent genius incomplete. The criticism, if such a thing there be, is didactic and aterpene, telling us nothing that we did not know, telling us all about everything that is plainly visible to half an eye; and telling us these aggravating things in a facile-natured, somewhat pedagogic, and ultimately exasperating manner. Of course the book is an almost unmitigated panegyric. Even the few passages that are not panegyrical are couched in the obvious and dulcet murmur which a grandfather would address to an exuberant grandson – e.g.:

The juvenile poet is too pictorial; his way of producing an image of lovely woman is by enumerating her charms; he describes beauty in detail as it might be painted, instead of describing its effects as the great poets, from Homer downward, are usually content to do. (p. 17.)

* *Tennyson*. By Alfred Lyall. – Ed.

Now a two-shilling Life of an English Man of Letters should be a manual, exhaustive in material, concise in form, exquisite and subtle in analysis, a manual which to the intelligent reader is a 'Life', a vivid presentment of an English 'Man' and of his 'Letters', containing all that is necessary to a knowledge of that Man and of his Work. Such a manual was Sir Leslie Stephen's *Johnson* in this same series. Such a manual Sir Alfred Lyall's *Tennyson* emphatically is not. He is diffuse on accidentals, mute on essentials; and at all times he employs 'a sententious phraseology instinctively, as men do when they are nervous, as well as when they justify the cynic's definition of the uses of speech'. He implies that everything about Tennyson has been written in the *Memoirs*. We cheerfully concede the point. He says that the few private and personal facts and incidents connected with Tennyson with which he favours us are taken direct from the *Memoirs*. But we deny his consequence. Sir Alfred has not taken enough, or of sufficient quality, from the *Memoirs* wherewith to compose a vivid picture of the Divine Laureate. The *Memoirs* are not easily accessible to all; and this Life ought to have been a compendium which would enable busy men to dispense with the said *Memoirs*. It is not. We are told the date and place of Tennyson's birth and death; the date of creation of his peerage; we are given a timid disquisition on his philosophy, on his religious views, his career at Cambridge, his excursions to the Pyrenees, Cornwall, Scilly, and Auvergne, his building operations, his shyness, his epigram on Jane Austen. His more delicious *mot*, describing the popular view of the *Padre Eterno* as An inmensurable Clergyman in a white Neck-Tie, is omitted, and his tobacco pipes are barely hinted at. The few details are doled out with such miserly stinginess that the personality of the Man, Tennyson, and therefore his talent also (for true talent, says Max Nordau, is always personal), remain for us the merest spectres. He is asomatose, living not, nor moving.

In the same way Tennyson the Poet suffers at Sir Alfred's hands. We learn that he once said

If I mean to make any mark in the world it must be by shortness, for the men before me had been so diffuse. (p. 36.)

We note that he listened to senile rustics for idiomatic phrases: studied, as a painter studies, that continuous system of Becoming

which men call Nature: meditated during miscellaneous half-hours
in a high-backed chair: polished his verses with intent assiduity.
We are treated to a very large number of excerpts as specimens of
his styles; and (not to deceive our readers) we may as well admit that
it was a contemplation of these excerpts which first set us pondering
why, in the name of all the Muses, the writing of this Life was
intrusted to Sir Alfred Lyall, or, if he wrote it on his own initiative
for his sole proper delectament, why the house of Macmillan have
published it. The critical acumen, the faculty of selection, which is
responsible for these excerpts, must be quite singularly inadequate.
Of course Tennyson is a mine of fastidiose expressions; and he must
be a true poet himself who would pretend to pick out the choicest.
However, Sir Alfred fails to recognize Tennyson as Buccinator
Novi Temporis in

> Ring out the Old, ring in the New.

He cites:

> Forward to the starry track,
> Glimmering up the height beyond me,
> On, and always on,

and neglects the pure cold crystalline radiance of St Agnes' Eve.
He cites:

> Sir Aylmer Aylmer, that almighty man,
> The county God,

and neglects:

> Bride of the heir of the kings of the sea,
>
> .   .   .   .
>
> For Saxon or Dane or Norman, we,
> Teuton or Celt, or whatever we be,
> We are each all Dane in our welcome of thee,
> Alexandra.

He cites:

> to guard thee in this wild hour coming on,
> lest but a hair of that low head be harm'd,

and neglects:

> musing on the little lives of men,
> and how they mar this little by their feuds.

read rascal in the motions of his back
and scoundrel in his supple-sliding knee.

and snake-like slimed his victim ere he gorged.
.   .   .   .

Worse remains. That bright gem 'The Victim' is not even named,
nor the grandiloquent Alcaics:

> O Mighty-mouth'd inventor of harmonies,
> O skill'd to sing of Time and Eternity,
> God-gifted organ-voice of England,
> Milton, a name to resound for ages;

nor the delicate Ithyphallics:

> Look, I come to the test, a tiny poem
> All composed in a metre of Catullus,
>
> .   .   .   .
>
> Hard, hard, hard, is it only not to tumble
> So fantastical is the dainty metre.

And there are other horrible exclusions. But the index is useful, as far as it goes; and the paper is very nice; and we rather fancy the flat-backed binding.

Tennyson died in 1892. That is ten years ago. His *Memoirs* and his *Works* we have, and these should suffice us – until we get him focussed in his proper perspective. Then it will be possible to include a Tennyson volume in a series of 'Lives of English Men of Letters'. That will be in or about the year 1992, and not a moment before.

Textual Notes

THE ARMED HANDS (p. 13)

This short story is referred to by Rolfe in a letter to Harry Pirie-Gordon dated from Oxford September 30th 1906: 'Please read *The Armed Hands*' and he mentions it elsewhere as a 'story surreptitiously printed 9th January last'. No trace has been found of the story's actual publication.

The MS., which is in the late David Roth's Martyr Worthy collection,* is on one side of eight leaves of quarto-sized paper, headed: 'Submitted by *Uriele de' Ricordi, 286 San Marco, Venice*. Price of English serial rights £17. 12. 6. stg cash'.

Although *The Armed Hands* was probably written in or before 1906, Rolfe later rewrote, or at least revised, it in Venice. The setting for the piece is Oxford, with which the author had had ties since his adolescence. It was there that he was an unattached student in the eighteen-seventies or eighties, later he was received there into the Catholic Church, and for a number of years he spent the summer in Oxford working for Dr E. G. Hardy, the Vice Principal of Jesus College. The character of the Grey Man is obviously founded on the author himself. Harry Pirie-Gordon refers to Rolfe wearing rings which, if necessary, he could use to defend himself against the Jesuits.

DAUGHTER OF A DOGE (p. 23)

This sketch appears here in print for the first time. Written as an independent piece, it represents the basis of Rolfe's opening chapter to his Venetian novel *The Desire and Pursuit of the Whole*. There are two MSS. One is in Donald Weeks's collection and does not include Rolfe's preamble in square brackets. This MS. is on one side of ten leaves of squared, foolscap paper, and headed 'Oct. 1/09. From Mr Rolfe, Palazzo Mocenigo Corner, Camp San Polo, Venezia. About 3000 words. Venetian words spelt in Venetian fashion'. The other MS., from which the present text is printed, is in the Martyr Worthy collection. Headed with the note 'Kindly keep my punctuation. R.', it is on one side of twelve leaves of foolscap paper.

* David Roth published an account of his Rolfe collection in *Desiderata*, February 4th 1955.

TEMPTATION (p. 33)

This sketch was published in four periodical instalments in *The Holywell Record* (June, July, August and October 1897) which Rolfe edited during its last six months. When the *Record* ceased publication, this serial story remained unfinished. It appeared below the name of 'John Blount', the joint pseudonym of Rolfe and John Holden. This is one of several pieces they wrote in collaboration: 'The better things were sighed "Corvo",' Holden later recalled: 'those more or less predestined to rejection were signed "Blount" '.

The character Geoffrey Lygon is clearly Rolfe and the story is almost certainly based on a personal experience. The reference on the opening page to his conversion 'nine years before . . . from high Anglicanism to the Catholic Faith', dates the episode as taking place in 1894 or early in 1895. Who Mrs Maltravers, Mrs Thompson, Deighton, or the unfortunate Johnnie Palmer were remains a mystery.

ARRESTED AS A SPY (p. 44)

This sketch appears here in print for the first time. The MS., which is in the Martyr Worthy collection, is on one side of thirteen leaves of quarto-sized paper.

Rolfe's arrest in Venice on suspicion of spying occurred on September 23rd 1909, while he was staying at Dr and Mrs van Someren's. He recounted it in a shorter form in two postcards sent to his friend Harry Pirie-Gordon on September 25th. This is one of several pieces describing experiences during the first eighteen months of his life in Venice. The reference to Count Luigi Sbrojavacca in the opening sentence indicates that, if this was written in the autumn of 1909, it was revised several years later. For the Count was Rolfe's landlord at the Palazzo Marcello where he lived from the spring of 1913 until his death in October of the same year. A note to Horatio Brown, on the back of the MS. of Rolfe's story *An Ossuary of the Lagoon*, now in Donald Weeks's collection, reads: 'Here is one of the fifteen things you advised me to write for the *Westminster Gazette*. Mr Spender as I mentioned refused them. Could you suggest another likely editor?' Three Venetian sketches were subsequently published in *Blackwood's Magazine*, but this is probably one of the remaining dozen which failed to see the light.

TOTO (p. 54)

This story appears here in print for the first time in its present form. It is in fact an early version of a story published in *The Pall Mall Magazine* for

May 1906 as *The Princess's Shirts*. The setting is Genzano-di-Roma where, following his expulsion from the Scots College in Rome, Rolfe spent some months in 1890–91 as a guest of the elderly English Duchess Caroline Sforza-Cesarini, who appears in the story as the Princess of Sant Angelo.

From the time Rolfe left Christchurch in 1892 until October 1956, the MS. of this story was preserved first by his landlord Mr Gardner and then his son; it was from the latter that I bought it eighteen years ago. The MS., which is in Rolfe's early, schoolmaster's hand, is written on one side of fifteen leaves of quarto-sized paper and belongs now to Donald Weeks, by whose courtesy it is printed today.

EXCOMMUNICATED: A HUMAN DOCUMENT (p.59)

This sketch appears here in print for the first time. No MS. version of it is known, but what appears to be Rolfe's typescript, on one side of fourteen leaves of quarto-sized paper, is now in the Martyr Worthy collection, and it is from this typescript that the present text is printed.

The piece illuminates and supplements our knowledge of Rolfe's life at Holywell. This is 'the town where I am used so scurvily', wrote Rolfe, 'where the hand of every man oppresses me, and where my hand is against every man's. It is the most bestially disagreeable place I ever saw'. Rolfe quarrelled with the parish priest of Holywell, Fr Charles Beauclerk – the 'one Jesuit' and 'The Reverend Carlos Belestudiante' of the present story – early in 1897; but, if the author's reference to himself being 'a Roman Catholic for thirteen years' is accurate, this story belongs to January 1899. By then Rolfe had retired into Holywell workhouse. The 'Prussian' of the story is Frank W. Hochheimer, the proprietor of *The Holywell Record*, referred to as 'our journal'. Another of Rolfe's Holywell sketches, *The Tattoed Wedding Ring*, almost certainly owes a good deal to the unfortunate Hochheimer.

IN PRAISE OF BILLY B. (p.70)

This story was published in *The Holywell Record*, July 31st 1897, pages 13–15. It appeared below the name of 'May Chester'. No MS. version of it is known. The aesthete Mr Simone Memmi Simpkinson and his saviour Billy B. have not been identified.

THE BULL AGAINST THE ENEMY OF THE ANGLICAN RACE (p.74)

This piece was privately printed in pamphlet form, edited by A. J. A. Symons from MSS belonging to himself and the Hon. Oliver Brett (later

Lord Esher), in 1929, in a limited edition of 50 copies. It was reprinted as an appendix to *The Quest for Corvo* (Cassell & Co., 1955). The Esher MS., written in red ink on one side of seven leaves of quarto-sized paper, belongs now to Donald Weeks, by whose courtesy it is printed today. Symons's MS. of *The Bull* subsequently passed to Sir Hugh Walpole and is now in the Bodleian Library (MS. Walpole c. 10).

This Bull is a violent attack upon Lord Northcliffe and *The Daily Mail*, written by Rolfe in his self-imagined role of Pope Hadrian VII. Symons was mistaken in saying that it was omitted from *Hadrian the Seventh* owing to its libellous content; in fact, the Bull was not written until the autumn of 1908.

Sir Shane Leslie has described Rolfe's Bull as 'the finest sequence of Corvine prose . . . It represented his dislike of the cheap Press and all the developments in Fleet Street during the nineties. His wrath took pontifical form and it is doubtful if the Latinists of the Roman Bullarium could have composed anything so sustained, furious, and magnificently medieval. It should figure in all future Literature of Hate' (*The Quest for Corvo*, 1955, p. 250).

NOTES ON THE CONCLAVE (p. 81)

This article was published in *The Monthly Review* (August 1903, pages 74–88), to which Rolfe was also contributing his series of 'Reviews of Unwritten Books'. No MS. version of it is known. Pope Leo XIII died on July 20th 1903. In April 1899, Rolfe had written an article on the same theme for the Sunday Magazine of *The New York World* entitled *When the Pope Dies*.

DANIEL ON THE COMING OF THE MESSIAH: FRAGMENT OF A DISCOURSE (p. 94)

This fragment was published in *Frederick Rolfe and Others* (St Albert's Press, Aylesford, 1961, pages 32–33). It was written during the short period Rolfe spent studying for the priesthood at the Scots College in Rome, in the latter part of 1889 and the early months of 1890. The curious story of how it survived is told by the late Canon Robert Carmont in a letter to A. J. A. Symons: 'I rescued from the waste-paper basket a portion of a paper [Rolfe] wrote at the behest of his professor of Scripture. It is in English and is of no intrinsic value. . . . I saw it not long ago and am in hopes of being able to produce it for you. Why I kept it these 44 years heaven only knows. I have done some curious things like that'.

Carmont was writing forty years ago. What has become of the original is not known, but a typescript made from it, presumably by either Carmont or Symons, is in the Bodleian Library (MS. Walpole d.14, folios 16 & 17), together with the original of the Canon's barbed recollections of Rolfe which Symons printed in *The Quest for Corvo*.

SUGGESTION FOR A CRITERION OF THE CREDIBILITY OF CERTAIN HISTORIANS (p. 96)

This article was published in *The Westminster Review*, October 1903, pages 402–414. No MS. version of it is known. It is in fact an amended version of Rolfe's appendix 3 to *Chronicles of the House of Borgia* (1901) which was set up in type but suppressed by the publisher.

THE VENETIANS (p. 111)

This article appears here in print for the first time. The MS., on one side of fifteen leaves of quarto-sized paper watermarked 1906, was formerly in the collection of J. Maundy Gregory and is now in the Martyr Worthy Collection. It has no title. From Rolfe's references to having lived in Venice for five and a half years (he went there in the summer of 1908) and the description of himself as 'a bigoted Roman Catholic of twenty-eight terrible years' standing' (he was received into the Catholic Church on January 3rd 1886), this is evidently one of his last writings.

CONCERNING ENGLAND AND GERMANY (p. 121)

This short article appears here in print for the first time in full, though the opening page of Rolfe's MS. was reproduced as an illustration in *The Quest for Corvo* (The Folio Society, 1952). The MS., on one side of five leaves of foolscap paper, was formerly in the collection of J. Maundy Gregory and is now in the Martyr Worthy collection. The date of composition is not known, but it was probably written about 1904.

THREE BOOK REVIEWS (p. 124)

These three reviews were published anonymously in *The Outlook*, October 18th 1902, pages 321–322, and February 21st 1903, pages 71–73. No MS. versions of them are known. Rolfe was at that time living at 69 Broadhurst Gardens, West Hampstead, and working on *Hadrian the Seventh*.